THE AUTHOR

Marion Miller has long been fascinated by the lives and exploits of the landowners of the North East, but her successful career running one of Scotland's most popular and distinctive tourist destinations, the Millers Visitor and Retail Centre in Aberdeenshire, prevented her from writing about them until now. She lives at Midmar, not far from Sir Alexander MacRobert's home on the Douneside Estate in Tarland. She has also been a well-known breeder of Border Leicester sheep. Today, when not digging in the archives, she enjoys a busy family life and turning a 'wilderness' into a garden and being joint president of Soroptimist International, Aberdeen.

Cawnpore to Cromar

The MacRoberts of Douneside

Marion Miller

Librario

Published by

Librario Publishing Ltd.

ISBN: 978-1-909238-09-1

Copies can be ordered via the Internet
www.librario.com

or from:

Brough House, Milton Brodie, Kinloss
Moray IV36 2UA
Tel/Fax No 00 44 (0)1343 850 178

I would like to thank all those who allowed me to use
photographs from their archives:
The MacRobert Trust for a great number of pictures both from India
and Scotland, Aberdeen Journals Ltd, Aberdeen City Libraries,
The RAF Museum/National Museum of Scotland,
The Martin R. Ford-Jones collection and Marianne More-Gordon
for a picture of her textile wall hanging.

Printed and bound in the UK

Cover Design: Monika Gromek

Front Cover Picture: Marianne More-Gordon

Typeset by 3btype.com

© Marion Miller 2014

This book is dedicated to the Trustees,
Administrators and staff, past and present,
of the MacRobert Trust

Contents

Author's Note   9
Introduction   11

Chapter 1   The Aberdeen Years   13
Chapter 2   Mills And Mutiny   21
Chapter 3   Dusters, Dances and Dangers   29
Chapter 4   Missions Of A Memsahib   39
Chapter 5   Farms, Families and Feuds   46
Chapter 6   The Delhi Durbar   55
Chapter 7   Levelling The Playing Field   62
Chapter 8   A Lasting Legacy   68
Chapter 9   Change And Chance   78
Chapter 10   Trials And Tribulations   87
Chapter 11   The Amir And Afghanistan   97
Chapter 12   Bringing It All Together   105
Chapter 13   Death Of A Merchant Prince   114
Chapter 14   A Band Of Brothers   124
Chapter 15   Godmother To The RAF   137
Chapter 16   Ladies At Loggerheads   146
Chapter 17   Looking After Her Ain   157
Chapter 18   A Job Well Done   163
Chapter 19   The Herds – Her Other Legacy   171
Chapter 20   An End And A Beginning   178

Acknowledgements   192
Bibliography   197
Index   199

Author's Note

When a baronetcy was conferred on him in 1922, Sir Alexander McRobert decided to change the family name to 'MacRobert'. I have used this spelling throughout this book, except when referring to Sir Alexander's parents and to the prizes, fellowships and buildings he endowed before then.

Introduction

The seeds of this book were sown in my childhood.

I grew up in a tenement in Aberdeen where my father worked as a cast iron dresser in a foundry. Mother, when not at her work in the City Library, could be found with her head buried in a book, oblivious to the tatties boiling dry and the dust accumulating thick and fast on the floors and furniture.

In common with my friends I enjoyed reading comics such as the Bunty, Beano and Dandy, but as I grew up I devoured every book I could lay my hands on about the great estates of North-East Scotland and the people who ran them. Tracking down these memoirs, biographies and statistical accounts became even easier after I left school and like my mother, worked at the City Library.

Much later, after retiring from my business, the Millers Visitor and Retail Centre in Aberdeenshire, which became one of Scotland's most popular and distinctive tourist destinations, I could at last return to the research that I had begun in my salad days.

At first I thought I would write a book in which each chapter would be devoted to one of the historic estates of the North East of Scotland, concentrating on the business activities of their Lairds and on the influence that the Lady of the House exerted over the local community. But after being given access to the archives of the MacRobert Trust, which is based right on my doorstep in the Deeside village of Tarland, I found a new focus.

The Trust is internationally known as one of Britain's major charities, but the extraordinary story of the three people whose work and vision created the fortune which founded it is less familiar and has never been fully told. As a businesswoman I was fascinated by how Sir Alexander MacRobert built up a huge fortune from beginnings that were very humble indeed, and as a mother, I was moved by the tragic circumstances which inspired his widow to devote her life and legacy to a uniquely spirited and imaginative brand of philanthropy.

This book interweaves three stories: of Sir Alexander's journey from his first home in a humble Aberdeen tenement to the highest echelons of the British Raj, thanks to his creation of a giant conglomerate the British India Corporation; of the Douneside estate on Royal Deeside in Aberdeenshire, where his second wife Rachel pioneered modern cattle-breeding and lobbied for youngsters and ex-servicemen to have the opportunity to find work in agriculture; and of how in her long widowhood, after the untimely deaths of her three sons, Rachel became a shining example in the face of adversity, taking on the Nazis in World War II by funding the purchase of five aircraft, one of which was named 'MacRobert's Reply', and perpetuating the memory of a great family in the important charity that today still bears its name.

But this is also a human story set between 1854 the year of Sir Alexander's birth and 1954, when Lady MacRobert died: a century of economic, social and political upheavals that changed the world for ever.

CHAPTER 1

The Aberdeen Years

A threefold cord is not easily broken. I trust that in the passing of the years, though men may come and men may go, there will always be a MacRobert at Douneside.

With those words, written from the Manse at Tarland in Aberdeenshire on 18 May 1917, the Reverend W. Marshall Low sent his congratulations to Sir Alexander MacRobert on the birth of his third son, Iain. Little was the good minister to know that fate would decree otherwise: for within thirty years, as a consequence of a series of tragedies, that cord would be severed.

He was not to know that the name would live on by other means: through buildings such as the MacRobert Arts Centre at Stirling University, the MacRobert buildings at Aberdeen University, and the MacRobert Pavilion at the Royal Highland Agricultural Society's showground at Ingliston near Edinburgh. The United Kingdom's premier award for outstanding innovation in engineering carries the MacRobert name as does 'MacRobert's Reply', an aircraft deployed with XV Squadron of the RAF. People throughout the country will come upon plaques commemorating the family name for a whole variety of reasons and wonder who they were.

Iain's death at the age of only twenty-four was the catalyst for the creation of the MacRobert Trust. He was the youngest of Sir Alexander's three sons. His eldest brother Alasdair had succeeded to the baronetcy of Cawnpore and Cromar when his father died in 1922, but he was killed when the plane in which he was flying crashed onto a wheat field near Luton airport in June 1938. The title then passed to Roderic, a serving officer in the RAF, who in his turn fell in action over Iraq in 1941. Iain, who was a pilot officer in Coastal Command, followed just four weeks later: he was presumed lost at sea during a search for a bomber crew that had ditched off Yorkshire.

Although the baronetcy, so briefly held, was now extinct and a potential dynasty had been brought so brutally to an end, the deaths of her sons marked a new beginning for their devastated mother. With remarkable resilience, spirit and courage, she immediately decided to carry on the fight for peace in their names.

Soon she was a public figure, known all over the country and further afield. But while the story of Lady MacRobert and her support of the RAF has often been told, less is known about the huge contribution she made, and continues to make, to many other aspects of British life through the charitable foundations she set up. And what of Sir Alexander? Blank stares usually accompany any mention of his name, yet he made the MacRobert fortune.

This son of Aberdeen came from a very humble background in the North East of Scotland, but he found success in a country far from his native land, as founder of the British India Corporation, one of the most important business conglomerates of the Empire. He chose his wives well, and both contributed to his many achievements. The first, Georgina, was a woman of true Christian spirit, much loved and respected in their adopted homeland of India. His second, Rachel, thirty years his junior and the mother of his three boys, was a woman of immense and indomitable character who triumphed over her own painful adversities to the continuing benefit of the wider world.

Sir Alexander's baronetcy was not the only honour accorded to him. In India he was esteemed as a Merchant Prince, in Britain as a Captain of Industry and he became much sought-after as an advisor to Governments and foreign rulers.

It was fortunate for 'Mac', as his Indian associates called him, that Aberdeen, the city where he was born, studied, and spent his early working life, was a centre for the manufacturing industries and that its textile businesses enjoyed a particularly good reputation.

Mac was born in 1854 to working class parents. For the first two weeks of his life the family lived in a tenement in Ann Street, Aberdeen, in the shadow of Richard & Company's mighty Broadford Mill. This was not a peaceful environment. Reputedly, it was 'one of the sights of the town to see the hands coming out at the gate at meal time'. The clamour created by around 2,000 pairs of feet of the workers who tramped over the cassies each day to spin and weave at the mill may well have woken the slumbering babe.

Richards and Co, working from what was to become an iconic, red brick building bordered by Hutcheon Street, Maberly Street, George Street, and Ann Street, was only one of the many companies that, from the 1600s, had pioneered the development of the textile industry in the city. Crombie Mills exported its fine tweeds and overcoats to Europe and America, and Alexander Hadden and Co. were leaders in innovation, using steam-driven engines to produce woollen garments for both the domestic and foreign markets. The firm also distributed wool to home spinners and knitters throughout the county, and despite being crafted in the most basic conditions, the stockings and gloves produced were of the very highest quality. It is said that a pair of the finest stockings manufactured in the city in about 1750 was presented by the City Council to Frederick the Great's Field Marshal, James Keith of Potsdam, who hailed from Aberdeenshire. Twenty-four miles of thread could be had from each pound of wool to make a stocking so fine that it could be drawn through a thumb ring. Not surprisingly, a pair of such superlative quality cost a phenomenal five guineas, or more than £600 in today's money.

Many of these firms were owned and operated by true entrepreneurs, intrepid men who seized every opportunity in those times of radical change to take advantage of new technology and the benefits of social reform. Never resting on their laurels, they made Aberdeen a prosperous city, one in which Mac was fortunate to grow up and spend the first years of his career. His own approach to business and social and moral responsibilities may well have been influenced by their practices, ethos and culture.

His diaries and notebooks show that his powers of observation were formidable and his thirst for knowledge keen. As a habitual writer of notes, he meticulously recorded the daily happenings of his life. These provide us today with an insight into his personality: not least evidence of his acute and enquiring mind.

When Mac was two weeks old, the family moved to a croft at Stoney-wood, the home of a famous paper mill. This was to play an important part in his life. Later, he attended the local school where Mr W.A. Williamson, his teacher, seems to have whetted his appetite for knowledge. So much so that, many years later, Mac contributed the then large sum of £100 to his mentor's retiral presentation. Mr Williamson may have been the first to recognise that Mac had an encyclopaedic brain and an outstanding ability to absorb information, attributes that others were to recognise and admire throughout his life.

When Mac was 12, like most young men who lived in that part of the city, he went to work at the mill. He started as a sweeper, a menial task befitting a working-class boy of that age in the mid 19th century. He may have worked alongside his father, for John McRobert supplemented his income from the croft by working there too. It also appears that at some time John was employed as a dairyman, giving him the knowledge he needed when, in later years, he emigrated to Canada to try his hand at farming.

The manufacturing capabilities of Stoneywood Paper Mills, housed in 30 granite buildings spread across 16 acres, were recognised worldwide and it was regarded as one of the greatest industrial establishments of its time. Its owner, 'Pirie of the Mill', was a cultured man and was reputed to have an exceptional collection of china and other fine art that was unrivalled in the area. Between 1850 and 1890, this dynamic and innovative company espoused the latest technology, increasing its workforce from 200 to 1,500 employees and contributing much to Aberdeen's prosperity.

Mac was not only to emulate this pioneering culture in future years when developing his own Cawnpore Woollen Mill, but, like Pirie, he also inspired and motivated his workforce. Both were concerned about the welfare of their employees and were pioneering advocates of social reform.

The Education (Scotland) Act of 1872 established a system of elementary education, but even before it was implemented, Pirie had founded a school at Stoneywood. The aim of the Act was to encourage people in parishes throughout the country to set up School Boards to operate educational establishments. These Boards also had the power to organise evening classes in vocational and non-vocational subjects. Thus, in the years that followed, Mac was not only able to study after work but also to conduct evening classes himself at Woodside in the city.

'Keep the demon of indolence at bay': so reads one of the many quotations recorded in Mac's notebooks. He certainly seems to have taken that one to heart, and throughout his life he appears never to have allowed himself an idle moment.

Aberdeen's city fathers had long realized the importance of encouraging its citizens to become skilled workers to meet the needs of its flourishing businesses. One result of the campaign they mounted was the Mechanics' Institute that was set up in 1824 to teach the fledgling disciplines of science and technology. Its courses were many and diverse, but it failed to run profitably and in the year of Mac's birth, its administrators seized the opportunity to replace it with a 'School of Science and Arts'. This venture, tried out for a year, was a success and in 1857 a new Technical School was also opened to cater for students pursuing careers in technical and mechanical draughtsmanship for the shipbuilding and engineering industries.

In Market Street, the Mechanics' Institute and the School of Science and Arts were joined for a short time by the School of Navigation. From 1872, these establishments began to provide further education to those who had left school at an early age. Mac attended and chose, it is said, to take no fewer than seventeen subjects, ranging from biology and history to psychology and the theory of music. That he passed in all of them is testimony to his abilities and to his eagerness to absorb knowledge, later described by the writer of his obituary in Calcutta's Statesman newspaper as 'an abiding passion'. As we shall see, he never lost this appetite for learning.

Another jotting in his notebook is a phrase taken from the Book of Ecclesiastes in the Bible: 'Whatsoever thy hand findeth to do, do with all thy might.' Mac's determination and stamina, his willingness to slog away at the most difficult tasks and his ability to remain focused and alert were exceptional, and as a reward for his endeavours, he was promoted to work in the office at the Mill.

In 1881, during a radical shake-up in the world of education, another famous Aberdeen establishment was also considering its future. Robert Gordon's Hospital had been set up for the 'maintenance, aliment, entertainment and education' of young boys whose parents could not afford to keep them at school. Now permission was granted to reorganise it as Robert

Gordon's College, and its teachers were given carte blanche to devise a curriculum of evening classes for adults covering a diverse range of topics. Nothing could have been more suitable for Mac.

These classes began in 1882, albeit on a small scale. Among the subjects on offer on the curriculum was chemistry, and even while continuing to work in the office, Mac seems to have acquired enough knowledge at evening classes to teach this subject at the college himself.

He also held the post of part-time lecturer in experimental physics at the Mechanic's Institute. This position had been created from a donation from Neil Arnott, an extraordinary man who managed to combine an outstanding career in medicine and another as an inventor. He gave generously not only to the academic institutions in Aberdeen but also to those in the other three cities in Scotland. Many years later, Mac was to have cause to be grateful to his ingenuity. When his first wife Georgina lay dying, he bought a waterbed invented by Arnott that helped to alleviate her pain.

After graduating in medicine at Marischal College, Aberdeen, Arnott went on to become a surgeon at the tender age of nineteen. He served in this capacity with the British East India Company before setting up a practice in London. He was highly respected and as a result, became physician to the French and Spanish embassies. In 1837 he was appointed physician extraordinary to Queen Victoria, joining the ranks of courtiers with North East connections, such as Sir James Reid and James Clark. Mac delivered the lectures at the Mechanic's Institute in Arnott's name.

In 1931, nine years after Mac's death, when his second wife Rachel spoke at the opening of the MacRobert Hall at Robert Gordon's, she said:

> I trust that the fullest use will be made of it, so that the benefits to the students may be in proportion to the conception of those who were first inspired by a sense of its need.

Meanwhile Mac's career in the paper industry flourished. He was transferred to the Union Works, located near the Joint Station in Aberdeen and part of the Stoneywood enterprise. This factory, where the first envelope-making machines were installed in 1913, became celebrated for producing 13,000,000 envelopes a week, which represented one third of the total made in Britain at the time. This new job seems to have been a position of responsibility, since Mac visited the mill at Stoneywood on a quarterly basis to audit the books. He is remembered by the young boys in the office as a subject of much hilarity due to his abrupt manner and dapper appearance.

Mac was also frugal, proudly boasting in later life about the length of time he had worn his toupee – thirty-seven years! He used every inch of paper in his notebooks, even writing sideways in the margins. One of the entries, dated 1878, states:

'Never buy anything you are not in immediate want of – Books especially.' But he was generous in his attitude to his fellow workers.

When Mac was honoured with a knighthood in 1910, he received a letter of congratulations from the Dhariwal Mill Indian staff which read:

> By the deep and unfailing interest you have always taken in our welfare, you have endeared yourself to every heart. ... You have always been good enough to do and have done everything that was required to ameliorate the condition of the Indian staff. ... We are provided with a very necessary and important institution – the school – which you have given us for the use of our children. ... We are provided with Pucca houses in place of the old mud quarters. You have favoured us with the grant of the system of bonus ...

In 1880, Mac took time off to visit his family which had emigrated to Canada to farm. Working the land figured in the backgrounds of both his parents. His mother was the daughter of a farmer from Banchory Devenick on the outskirts of Aberdeen and his father John came from a large family born in the parish of Drumblade in Aberdeenshire.

John was content to stay at home, while three of his brothers emigrated to Australia in search of a better life. However, now with a wife and family to provide for, John and Helen were attracted by the prospect of a better way of life. Thus they undertook the long journey to New Brunswick, Canada, along with their six daughters and youngest son who was also called John. Mac had not been tempted to go with them, but when he visited them he was pleased to find that they were all gainfully employed and successful in their endeavours as pioneer farmers of the west. He returned from his trip with his observations on the country recorded meticulously, but still with no desire to join the family.

The following year, he was granted unpaid leave to attend lectures and do practical scientific work at the South Kensington Museum in London. There, in his constant pursuit of knowledge, he studied the mysteries of compound pendulum apparatus. The other observations in his journals covered subjects as diverse as the clothes worn by gentlemen in the capital and Gladstone's prowess as an orator.

Soon after his return to Aberdeen, Mac met Georgina Porter who also worked at the envelope factory but later left to manage the Claremont Laundry in the city. Georgina's mother, Christina, had struggled to bring up her family after her father George had gone to the Fraser River in British Columbia to prospect for gold and never returned. Georgina had two sisters, Annie and Mary, and a brother, William. So close was the relationship between Georgina and her mother, that many years on, Christina's body was exhumed and buried alongside Mac and Georgina in Allenvale cemetery in the city, close by the River Dee.

The couple fell in love and were soon making plans for the future. Mac applied successfully for a job as a chemist at the Muir Mill in Cawnpore, India, and they were married on 31 December 1883. When Mac set off alone for India early in the New Year, neither can have imagined that they were about to form another, equally enduring relationship: this time with a country and its people.

CHAPTER 2

Mills and Mutiny

All subsequent industrialisation (of Cawnpore) stemmed from … the genius of Gavin Jones and the stability of Hugh Maxwell and the man who was the most remarkable of all, the man who was to take over the mantle from Gavin Jones and become the uncrowned King of Cawnpore, Sir Alexander McRobert.

How did a clerk from an envelope factory in Aberdeen come to merit this accolade taken from Zoe Yalland's *Boxwallahs*, the authoritative account of the British presence in Cawnpore between 1857 and 1901?

The India Mac found on his arrival certainly lived up to its reputation: this was indeed a land of opportunities. Now that the scars left by the horrific massacre at Cawnpore during the Indian Mutiny thirty years before were healing, Cawnpore was in the throes of industrial expansion. Technicians, as they were described at that time, were much sought-after to assist in the development of the emerging industries. Yet his first experience of the place did not bode well.

We can only imagine what Mac must have felt when he was greeted by William Cooper of Cooper Allen, the managing agents for the mill. Cooper confessed that an unfortunate misunderstanding had occurred between those who had promised him a job as chemist at the Muir Cotton Mills: it had already been filled. Since they were all too aware that Mac had left his new bride and the relative security of his employment in North East Scotland to travel across the world to a job that now did not exist, the embarrassed Board of Directors at Cooper Allen endeavoured to find him another position.

Fortunately for Mac, the firm also managed the ailing Cawnpore Woollen Mill, which had been established in 1876. The business had changed its name when the New Indian Companies Act came into being in 1882, adding '& Army Cloth Manufacturing Co Ltd'. This was a public company and three of its Directors, George Allen, William E. Cooper, and Gavin Jones, became some of the most inspirational pioneers of industry and commerce in Cawnpore.

Jones, whose family had been associated with India since the late 1700s but had lost its fortune when the Union Bank of Calcutta failed in 1847, was said to have been influential in setting up every factory in Cawnpore at that time. Allen, who went to India in about 1850 to work in his family's business, played a vital role as a volunteer during the Mutiny. He organised runners who carried communications for the British authorities and also produced a news sheet, an experience that stood him in good stead when he started up the *Pioneer*, now one of India's national newspapers. As its proprietor, he was a man who could exercise considerable influence. And in later years he never allowed anyone to forget that he had brought not only Alexander MacRobert to India, but also Rudyard Kipling, who worked as the assistant editor at the Pioneer from 1887 to 1889.

Later, Georgina took his youngest son Charles T Allen under her wing, while another son, George Berney Allen, became Mac's closest friend and confidant. Indeed, while Rachel was giving birth to Iain in Scotland, Mac was nursing George in England during his final illness. A third son, HD Allen, (Harry) was to contribute much to Cawnpore life.

William Cooper also became a lifelong friend. Born into a farming family who hailed from Lincolnshire, he was encouraged by his mother to seek work in India, where in 1861 he found employment on an indigo estate. Eighteen years later he had moved to Cawnpore where he and George Allen set up Cooper Allen and Co. The firm consequently became managing agents at the Cawnpore Woollen Mill.

Since the mill used only the most basic equipment – a single mule and two power looms – it could only manufacture policemen's greatcoats and blankets from the coarse country wool intended for the home market. Predictably perhaps, the company did not trade profitably, and the chances that Mac might be able to turn it around were slim, especially as, when asked if he knew anything about wool, he replied with typical honesty, 'No, but I can learn'. Cooper Allen, in truth, had nothing much to lose: the mill was in serious decline, struggling to avoid bankruptcy.

Mac accepted the challenge and got the job. He drew on his studies and his experience of working in Aberdeen to examine all aspects of the business and then formulate a business plan. It is clear from his notes that he began by analysing how well the products produced by the mill fulfilled the demands of the market place. He also carefully assessed his competitors, the supply of raw materials, the mill's operating costs, the labour supply and the available channels of distribution. But there were other, more elusive, obstacles to overcome. Success would depend on understanding the ideas and modus operandi of Cawnpore's businessmen and the cultural and economic changes that had occurred since the Indian Mutiny.

The Mutiny had taken place in and around Cawnpore about thirty years before Mac arrived in the city.

After all the terrible atrocities, enduring harm had been done to the relationship between castes and between Indians and Europeans.

When the British East India Company was set up in 1600, Queen Elizabeth I of England granted it a Royal Charter to carry out trade with the East. Its remit grew, and its extensive powers developed over the years until it virtually ruled the country. Years of tax burdens, virtual slave labour and the monopoly of trade routes kindled resentment, and grievances, both social and political, had built up over the years. The annexation of land was a particular bone of contention: it had been the heritable property of generations of Indian rulers but had now been taken over by what were seen to be middle class British merchants.

A combination of all these factors led to a breakdown in trust and on to a bloody rebellion. At its height about 1,000 Europeans took shelter in General Wheeler's encampment at Cawnpore. There they survived the attacks on them for twenty-one days before becoming the victims of the Nana Sahib, an Indian leader who had originally declared allegiance to the British, but then went back on his word.

In one of the Mutiny's worst atrocities, the men were slaughtered in front of their families. When the rebel Sepoys refused to shoot the women and children, they were threatened with execution. A posse was forced to butcher them and the bodies of the dead were thrown into a well along with the handful of people who were still alive. In later years, as a lasting tribute to those who were slaughtered, a statue of an angel known as the Angel of the Well was erected in the Memorial Well Gardens in Cawnpore.

Gavin Jones was the joint owner of the Cawnpore Woollen Mill. His family owned an indigo estate at Fatehgarh which was situated about seventy-five miles north of Cawnpore in an area fraught with danger for European settlers. In an attempt to escape an attack by the rebels, a party of British people including Jones and some members of his family, set out for Cawnpore by boat. En route, they were attacked from the river bank. Some of the group opted to continue to Cawnpore where they perished in the massacre there, but forty members of the party decided to place their trust in a friendly Zemindar, as the land owners were called. He led them to a safe place in the jungle, but they were eventually forced back to defend the Fort at Fatehgarh. Though they fought fiercely, their heroic efforts failed and they had to flee to the river where most of them were slaughtered.

After seeing his brother shot in the head and then his sister-in-law and niece set upon and killed by the frenzied mob, Jones miraculously escaped. He was wracked with fever, burnt, blistered, covered with festering wounds and traumatised by the memories of the horrific slaughter of his brother and his family: the physical and mental anguish he suffered can hardly be imagined. Another friendly Zemindar came to his rescue. He and his villagers gave Jones shelter and helped him to recover from his ordeal. On hearing that Cawnpore had been recaptured from the rebels, he asked to be guided through the jungle to the river, where he rejoined a small party of his fellow countrymen and set out in another attempt to reach the city. This journey too was fraught with danger. When they eventually arrived, Jones's almost incredible survival caused amazement. His immense bravery earned him the Mutiny Medal.

Despite the destruction of property and the damage to its infrastructure, Cawnpore enjoyed rapid growth and economic prosperity after the uprising was quelled. This was due in large part to the efforts of entrepreneurs like George Allen, William Cooper, and Gavin Jones. Their understanding of Indian culture, history and politics, improved relations between the British and the local inhabitants. Soon the flourishing town was known as 'the Manchester of the East'.

These pioneers had their faults, however. Relationships between the businessmen who developed industry in the area were almost incestuous, nepotism was rife and there was always the threat that they would form cartels, making it difficult for any outsider to succeed in business. They seized their chances wherever possible, especially those presented by conflicts, wars and political situations. However, they did too, have a genuine interest in the welfare of their workers and a true desire to improve the lot of those whose country this was.

Some of the companies they formed were destined to become part of Mac's massive business empire, but this incomer from Scotland soon made life-long friends from amongst their ranks and wasted no time in infiltrating their circle and even outwitting them.

Many of those seeking good fortune in India at the end of the 19th Century were attracted to Cawnpore because it was so obviously a thriving industrial town in the throes of expansion. Mac must have found that the Cawnpore Mill looked similar to Broadford's and Stoneywood Mills back in Aberdeen with its chimneys that stood like sentinels over the city, belching forth smoke. Hooters sounded and a myriad Indian voices clamoured over the clatter of the machinery. Though they stood in the glaring unrelenting sunshine of India, in striking contrast inside, they were indeed dark, satanic mills, creating conditions which Mac worked hard to improve.

When Mac took the helm, the mill employed a small staff comprising a manager, an accountant, an engineer and a dyer and finisher. Mac's willing-ness to turn his hand to many of the practical tasks required of workers in the mill and his own understanding of the manufacturing processes, immediately put the company in a stronger position. By working long hours, especially in the early days, Mac became less reliant on his workers. But this did not stop him from using his charm and powers of persuasion to encourage them to lend the company as much as they could. He returned it in full when the company was no longer in dire financial straits, but without any interest. Canny Scot that he was!

One of Mac's first tasks was to create a brand name for the company. Just inside the perimeter of the mill compound where he lived and worked, there stood a Tamarind, or Lalimli tree. It was unique in that it bore red flowers rather than the common yellow variety. He adopted the name

Lalimli and this trade mark soon became synonymous with the garments the mill produced. He then embarked upon a concerted marketing campaign. In his advertisements he promised quality, telling prospective buyers that the company had 'nothing to do with cotton or shoddy or any other inferior fibre' and proclaiming, 'Everything is made from pure, sound wool. Only the very best of dyes are used and all colours and shades are as fast and permanent as they can be made.'

Thus states the Lalimli Dictionary, which Mac produced for new employees and clients. This shows that in just a few years under his management, he had revived the mill's fortunes. Mac was a master salesman and on reading the book, anyone contemplating doing business with Cawnpore Woollen Mill must have been impressed.

The claims grew ever bolder. One reassured buyers that 'Proprietors are British and every operation in every department is closely and personally superintended by highly trained British experts recruited from Yorkshire, the West of England and Scotland'; another confidently asserted that the mill was unique in that 'it is the only manufacturer in the world turning out 'anything made from wool'.

Soon, from modest beginnings, the Mill had diversified its range of products until only a small proportion of its output was devoted to blanket production. Although quality was of paramount importance, the Mill seems to have produced vast quantities of goods:

> The Company has ample financial resources allowing them to purchase any extent of raw materials to the best advantage for cash. This and the magnitude of the manufacturing operations, account for the phenomenally low prices at which they sell the finished all wool materials.

Although the after-effects of the Indian Mutiny and the abolition of the East India Company did begin to fade, another military campaign was to have an impact on the Mill and its fortunes. In 1885, shortly after Mac took up the reins at the Mill, the skirmish between the Afghans and the Russians at Pendjeh caused consternation in India. Afghanistan was strategically important because it acted as a buffer zone between Russia and India. From the early 1800s, the two Empires, Russia and Britain, engaged in espionage, diplomatic tactics and reconnaissance sorties in Afghanistan; a subtle war which was romanticised by Kipling in his novels and became known as 'The Great Game'.

In the first Afghan war in the 1830s, the British had attempted to impose a regime on the country but they were humiliatingly defeated. When the second war in the 1870s saw some 40,000 soldiers deployed to Afghanistan to see off a potential threat from the Russians, the fledgling businesses in Cawnpore provided the kit for Queen Victoria's army. Some of it was waterproof, made of an innovative new fabric invented by one of the Directors of the Muir Mill.

Since that time, Imperial Russia had advanced steadily, expanding its territories and posing a potential threat to India and the Empire by means of invasion through the Khyber Pass. In an attempt to keep the Russians at bay, the Amir had come to an arrangement with the Indian government for it to supply the Afghans with arms and ammunition. In return, the Amir allowed a degree of control over Afghanistan's foreign affairs.

Although the incident at Pendjeh was eventually solved by diplomatic means, it saw the loss of some 600 Afghans to their Russian adversaries. While this 'frontier scuffle' (as it was described by the Amir) was taking place, a conference was being held at Rawalpindi which the Amir of Afghanistan and Lord Dufferin, the Viceroy, both attended.

Also present was Mac. He was there in a bid to secure a contract to provide the army with extra supplies. The Indian government, fearing that Russia would invade Afghanistan leaving India vulnerable, thought it prudent to increase its complement of soldiers by about 23,000.

Mac's account in his diaries and journals of his meetings with a Colonel Parker as he embarked on his selling campaign, reveals a sense of humour as well as business acumen. Mac convinced the Colonel that if he dealt with the Mill, the army would benefit greatly. The Colonel never seems to have suspected that some of Mac's suggestions, while apparently made in the interests of the army, were born of purely selfish reasons. One was that the soldiers' pyjamas should be coloured khaki and not blue as the Colonel wished. Only Mac knew that the Mill did not have facilities to dye cloth blue at the time. Cunning ploys like this helped Mac to secure an order for thousands of garments and blankets with the promise of more to come.

The 'Lalimli Dictionary' boasted that one of the company's strengths was an ability to 'clothe an army in an incredibly short space of time.' Although the Mill worked at full capacity round the clock, Mac, who was himself working 18-hour days, soon realized that they could not fulfil the order. So to increase production Mac purchased the New Egerton Mill in the Punjab, which had been established by a Christian missionary in about 1880. When Mac made this first foray into business ownership, New Egerton employed 908 people, producing 'woollen worsted and hosiery of all kinds' and were sole manufacturers of the celebrated 'Dhariwal' long life wool wear. This solved his production problems and also eliminated a competitor.

The immediate future of the Cawnpore Mill was secured, and since shares in the company were cheap, Mac bought them whenever he could. As they gained in value, his wealth accumulated. Soon he was boasting:

'Primarily the Company lay themselves out for the production of Army cloths, serges and blankets. They have repeatedly earned and received the thanks of government for patriotic and invaluable assistance in times of emergency.'

Mac was careful not to keep all his eggs in one basket and set about expanding the business. By 1887, only three years after he took up the reins, he had transformed the business into a diverse manufacturing company employing over 2,000 workers. By 1904, in addition to supplying the army, the company had branched out into catering for the needs of the domestic and leisure markets too. On offer were garments and goods from the practical to the decorative, spun from a variety of materials – from serges to silk, from worsted to braid and felt. Lines included blankets for babies and horses, jerseys for polo players and footballers, church seating, putties, slouch hats, carpets and doormats. Sometimes when the tailoring department was not busy, it was called in to mend the frugal Mac's clothes. The list of goods and garments produced by the Mill reflects how the people of the Empire occupied their leisure time

At Cawnpore, social activities were many and varied, and Mac appreciated that a wife was a great asset to a businessman who was expected to entertain and be entertained. He began work on a bungalow and sent for Georgina to join him. Thus, at the end of 1885, she arrived in Cawnpore to take up residence at The Sheiling.

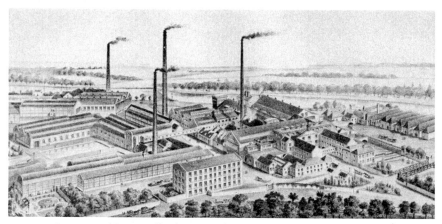

Stoneywood Papermill where Mac began his working life as a sweeper at the age of twelve.
(Aberdeen City Libraries)

The Cawnpore Woollen Mill where Mac began his career in India.
(The MacRobert Trust)

The offices at the Cawnpore Woollen Mill. Mac rescued the firm from bankruptcy.
(The MacRobert Trust)

Workers pose for the camera at the Mill.
(The MacRobert Trust)

Mac and his first wife
Georgina taken in 1886
the year after her arrival
in India.
(The MacRobert Trust)

The sitting room at the Shieling, the MacRoberts' home in Cawnpore.
(The MacRobert Trust)

Mac's father John MacRobert and Mac's brother Johnny at Burnside, Tarland, 1891.
(The MacRobert Trust)

Georgina's body lies in Allenvale cemetery, Aberdeen, alongside her mother and Mac.
(The Author)

Rachel and Mac on their wedding day, July 1911.
(The MacRobert Trust)

The newly extended Burnside (Douneside), June 1915.
(The MacRobert Trust)

Rachel did her bit for the nation and produced three sons, Alasdair, Roderic and Iain.
(The MacRobert Trust)

CHAPTER 3

Dusters, Dances and Dangers

To live in India, one must have an acute sense of humour and no sense of smell!

This was one of many witty observations by the Scottish novelist Anna Masterton Buchan who wrote under the pen name 'O. Douglas'. Georgina soon learned for herself how true it was.

What smells must have assailed Georgina's nostrils when she finally arrived in Bombay in 1885.

While growing up in Aberdeen, she would have been no stranger to the stench from sewers. A report in 1865 revealed that 'in two thirds of the city, (Aberdeen) had no sewers and that foul drainage found its way down open channels in the streets to the nearest stream or sewer grating.' In the middle of the century the cess pools and ash pits in these areas were uncovered and offensive: solid matter was carted away only periodically by scavengers. The Aberdeen Corporation Act of 1881 enabled the Council to begin clearing areas of the city where the worst of the pollution occurred, and in the year Mac went to India, the city's first large scale slum clearance finally got underway. This helped reduce the incidence of infectious diseases – and the stench.

Used as she may have been to the open sewers of Aberdeen, nothing could have prepared Georgina for the teeming mass of humanity, the noise, the heat and the flies, and the abject poverty of Bombay when she disembarked after her long journey. In India, she was to encounter deadly diseases such as smallpox and rabies, see lepers in the streets, and witness the devastation and heartbreak caused by the plague. Uprooting herself from Aberdeen brought her face to face with a culture and a life completely outwith her ken: this would have been a true test of her strength of character.

It was just as well perhaps that Cawnpore was in the United Provinces. This, according to one commentator of the age, was one of the more

salubrious parts of India and more accommodating to expatriates from
Europe:

> The United Provinces is in many respects a most attractive country. Its
> people are intelligent, hard working and prosperous and for the most
> part peace loving. Its climate is for the greater part of the year excellent,
> and in the hot weather one can retreat easily into the high Himalayan
> country with its glorious scenery.

Now, in November 1885, Mac and Georgina were united at last. Georgina
was joining that band of intrepid women who followed their men
throughout the Empire in search of a better life. With the army contract
secured and the mill beginning to prosper, they could face the future in
India with optimism.

Although she was delighted to see her husband again after so long apart,
Georgina had to admit to being disappointed with her new abode, The
Sheiling. Perhaps she had hoped for more, since they had stopped off with
the Allens in their lovely old home in Allahabad en route to Cawnpore
from Bombay.

Sir George Allen was, along with William Cooper, the other half of Cooper
Allen. As we have seen, he was an influential man with the ear of those in
authority in the United Provinces. His family business of Peake, Allen and Co
described itself in an advertisement placed in the *Pioneer* on 14 August 1876
as 'Dispensing and Operative Chemists, Manufacturers of Aerated Waters and
Perfumery; Importers of Patent Medicines, Surgical Instruments and Medical
Appliances, Veterinary Stores and Implements.' Over the years, Sir George
increased his fortune by buying out the other shareholders.

Perhaps it was not surprising that The Sheiling could not compare with
the well-appointed home of a man who was long-established and successful
in India, but Georgina was disappointed nonetheless. She wrote in her diary:

> My first impression of the house was anything but pleasant, as trades
> people were working on it and the rooms had a bare cold look.

It would have been out of character for Mac to have not made sure that
everything was ship-shape for Georgina's arrival. He had, after all, been
separated from his new bride since soon after their marriage on the last day

of 1883. She in her turn set about converting that 'bare cold house' into a warm and friendly home. Photographs taken later show rooms that have benefited from a woman's touch: they are decorated with pretty drapes and cushions, photographs and pictures on the walls, side tables and an abundance of knickknacks. Georgina had created a really cosy feel.

The hospitality at The Sheiling was to become renowned and the door was always open, even to sick people. A story oft told about Georgina's true Christian spirit dates from the time when a shortage of hospital beds for Europeans prompted her to nurse a stranger suffering from smallpox in her own home.

Yet Georgina had a lot to learn about life in India, both domestically and socially. There is no doubt that her sweet nature and kindness helped her make new friends with Mac's business associates and their wives. She took pains too, to forge good relations with the servants. Perhaps the greatest challenge that Georgina faced in her role as memsahib of The Sheiling was speaking the local language. Mac took the trouble to learn it, but surprisingly, Georgina seems never to have made the effort. And although she will have welcomed having servants, their presence in the house meant there was never any privacy. Her position as manageress of the Claremont Laundry in Aberdeen, might have given her experience in handling staff, but it did not prepare her for coping with the caste system and with the culture of the people she now had to rely upon for the smooth running of her household.

One of the banes of her life seems to have been the servants' all-consuming passion for dusters. Most memsahibs seem to have felt the same, finding the theft and misuse of this basic household necessity trying in the extreme.

'I try to get the men to be cleanly in their habits and to use the towels, dusters etc. I give them daily only for the purposes I name,' she wrote. But her efforts went unrewarded: 'still you will find them occasionally using one duster for all and it does annoy one so.' *Jharans*, as the servants called them, could be used for wrapping up and concealing pilfered food, as footballs, or as handkerchiefs and *rumals*, a kerchief worn as a headdress. Their disappearance and consequent replacement made a big hole in the memsahib's household budget.

31

Georgina also bemoaned the servants' dishonesty in her letters home. In one she complained: 'they lie so much it really is impossible to find out the truth about anything, and the poor cat is invariably taxed with all the breakages.' In another she made no secret of her frustration:

> I have something like 60 fowl of one sort or another just now, yet I only get a few eggs occasionally. The sweeper steals them as soon as they are laid, then sells them to the cook, who in turn sells them to me, as if he had bought them for cooking purposes from the bazaar … One must grin and bear it and make the best of them for they have some good qualities after all.

One of the challenges faced by expatriates in India was the weather. They found the heat and humidity in the rainy season hard to cope with. Even in the bungalow, Georgina wrote, the temperature could reach 98F in the morning:

> Everyone feels lethargic. The liver doesn't perform adequately in the heat and the damp and the body fills with bile.

Even the chickens succumbed to the heat:

> I have another seven hens sitting on eggs, many of the chickens will die, the heat kills them off. I suppose they can be kept alive, but it takes one some time to find out how to treat sick cats, dogs, horses and fowls in this country.

Although she had been brought up in a city, she enjoyed tending the animals.

> I spend lots of time seeing the horses groomed, animals fed, etc. It is always something to do, and the beasts get to love one so.

Like many women of means in Britain in that era, Georgina created a garden which ultimately ran to about five acres. This became a haven from the fierce heat and the dust from the mill, the constant yack of the looms and the clamour of the factory hooter calling the workers or signalling the end of a shift. Here they could partake of Tiffin under the shade of the trees and perhaps dream of the greenery of home.

When she returned from visits to Scotland, Georgina made sure that tucked into the corners of her suitcase, were packets of seeds to be sown in the garden at The Sheiling. She found that both root and salad vegetables thrived in the heat of India just as well as they did in Britain.

In a letter to their folks at Douneside, she was enthusiastic and just a little proud of her efforts as a gardener:

> Our new vegetables are coming on well; we have turnips, carrots, beetroot, tomatoes, radish, celery, lettuce, cress and a few other well known seeds, also a fine crop of peas.

Occasionally, in her diaries, Georgina recorded that Mac, or Alec as she called him, did not always give her gardening efforts the support she felt they deserved:

> I have been much upset today. A tree shaded the office grass so that it could not grow and I told Heera to take it up, telling Alec I had done so. In going over to the office he came upon them cutting down the tree and beat him on the head. Heera came to me as he was only obeying orders and told me. I went over and saw Alec, and said I did not think it quite right to beat a defenceless coolie because he was doing what he was told, and Alec was so angry with me, he said I ought to be ashamed of myself the way I got on. I think it unjust and it hurt me ... How I try to save him trouble and worry, it always seems in vain.

She went on to complain that the garden party she had organised that week had gone off well, thanks to her meticulous planning but without any help, or apparently thanks, from her husband. These were but minor blips in a very happy marriage.

Yet there were other dark entries in her diaries. In 1901 she wrote:

> I suppose I am not in good tone today, but my heart is sore. I wonder why God does not take me home. I suppose I am not ripe yet.

Was this her first intimation of the illness that was to kill her at an early age?

According to tributes paid after her death, Georgina inspired affection. Her servants loved 'Mother Georgie', and her friends praised her for her patience and sweetness.

In facing all these challenges in her new life, Georgina was fortunate to make the acquaintance of Nell Kirkman. Nell, affectionately known as 'Kirkie' or 'Little Nell', became a close and lifelong friend. She was married to a partner in Ford and MacDonald, a firm of construction engineers, and hailed from Nairn, a town less than 100 miles from Aberdeen, Georgina's own birthplace.

Kirkie was one of the 'senior' ladies in the business community in Cawnpore and she took Georgina under her wing. She taught her the rules of protocol and etiquette, how to dress and entertain, and what would be required of her as a society hostess and the wife of an up-and-coming businessman like Mac.

On 26 November, three days after her arrival in Cawnpore, Mac introduced his wife to the Butterworths. Alfred Butterworth was the Cawnpore Woollen Mill manager and he and his wife Polly had seven children. When their youngest daughter Ruby was born, Georgina begged to be allowed to adopt her. Georgina's inability to conceive was a continual source of disappointment. Her plea, of course, was refused but Ruby was given the second name Georgina. Another daughter, Kitty, later married Mac's nephew Arthur Lilley. Georgina would have been pleased: she thought Alfred and Polly 'very nice people'. At that first meeting, Georgina accompanied Polly on a drive and afterwards she wrote that she had enjoyed it very much. From then on her integration into the community was swift.

Yet, although she came to love India, she took time to settle and was constantly homesick. Even three years after her arrival she was writing:

This place is not home but we have been well and very happy here so we must be content to bear its ills too.

With Georgina at his side, Mac could now take a full part in social life in Cawnpore. The saying goes that all work and no play make Jack a dull boy and Mac and Georgina seemed to play as hard as they worked.

In those days, it was common for the larger mills to have social clubs where their staff could enjoy a bit of relaxation after work. Mac set up the Lalimli Club within the Cawnpore Woollen Mill compound, and here he enjoyed the company of his employees. It was testament to his character that he could socialize with them and still command their respect.

His men regarded him as a strong disciplinarian but they always thought him fair. He had clearly taken two of the numerous maxims recorded in his notebook to heart:

Never be slow to admit you are in the wrong. Make the confession without grudge or condition.

And,

Do not criticise – guard against the inclination to correct people.

The Lalimli club was the venue for the party Mac and Georgina held every year to celebrate both Hogmanay and their wedding anniversary. In fact, every birthday and anniversary was an excuse for a 'do' for those far from home in Cawnpore. The women were kept busy organising picnics for the children and 'get to know you' gatherings for newcomers. Everyone made merry at garden parties and dinners and the annual children's Christmas party, when each child received a gift imported from Britain, was eagerly anticipated.

The community's social life revolved around the Cawnpore Club and the Cawnpore Volunteers' Club. Photographs taken at the events they held show the men sporting pristine whites, the women immaculately dressed, often accompanied by the family dog and their house boys who sat at their feet.

While the more active enjoyed pastimes such as archery and croquet, the less energetic among them could engage in more sedentary pursuits like billiards. The dramatic society catered for those inclined to the arts, while residents could show off their talents at soirées, which were held regularly. Businessmen met there too, but Georgina especially enjoyed the competitions run by the flourishing tennis club and its annual 'at home' when, after the serious business was over, a veritable feast was consumed.

The many balls and dances where soldiers garrisoned at Cawnpore met young ladies visiting their relations in the area, provided an ideal opportunity for romance to flourish. While a military band played softly in the background, the company partook of cakes and sweets and many other delicacies, washed down with cherry brandy and claret cup. As daylight faded and the moon came up, dancing began: the ambience was perfect for romantic dalliances. Georgina took quite a few young men under her wing and no doubt dispensed advice to the lovesick too.

One keen observer of Indian society, the novelist Anna Masterton Buchan wrote that it was made up of 'Government people, army people and business people, or Boxwallahs as they are known.' Cawnpore was no exception, and the Army and the business community seem to have mixed. The soldiers were passionate about horse racing and the Cawnpore community enjoyed many an outing to watch the thrills and spills.

The Cawnpore Tent Club, though, was a male preserve. Its members were influential men from many sectors of the community: business and commerce, engineering and the police force, to name but a few. There they could network and make business contacts. The prime purpose of the club was the hunting of wild boar, or pig sticking as it was commonly called. Oddly this activity, enjoyed by so many men, was regarded as a stress-buster, despite the considerable risks involved and the constant danger of goring and even death presented by creatures that had grown big and mean on a diet of sugar cane and lush vegetation.

Visiting dignitaries were often invited to the Cawnpore meets, providing the townspeople with further opportunities to get to know influential people. The regimental band was in much demand to play at these events.

Much of Mac's free time was taken up serving in the Cawnpore Rifle Club which, along with the Cawnpore Light Horse made up the Cawnpore Volunteer Corps. Their mottos were, 'Forewarned, Forearmed', and 'Defence not Defiance' respectively. The Corps was akin to the Territorial Army in Scotland. Again, we can find similarities between Mac's life in India and his days in Aberdeen. There, long before Mac's time, another textile mill owner named James Hadden served as Lieutenant Colonel of the Royal Aberdeen Volunteers, an organisation formed to protect the city in the event of an enemy attack on Britain.

In Cawnpore, there was competition amongst the Mills to see which could muster the most men to serve. Mill owners played their part too and the most able volunteers assumed ranks which they used in civilian life. GB Allen was an Adjutant and Alfred Butterworth, the Mill manager, was a Colonel. Mac commanded the Volunteer Rifles from 1899–1912, with the rank of Lieutenant Colonel. In later years, he was given this rank when his second marriage was announced in an American newspaper.

Formed as a reaction to the events of the Mutiny, the Rifles aspired to have a body of men trained to support the police and army should a crisis arise. Club members were mostly English, but there were also Anglo-Indians in the ranks.

Training was provided by a military man who put the men and their horses through their paces. The mock battles fought with neighbouring units were regarded as light-hearted recreation even though they were fiercely fought. Other activities at these events included cutting an apple with a sword and a surviving photograph immortalises the Cawnpore Light Horse team that won the All India tent pegging competition in 1901. Trophies were awarded to those with the best military skills and the club-house was resplendent with silverware won in shooting matches and mock battles by teams that were supported by loyal bands of followers.

The skills of the Volunteer Rifles were put to the test in 1900. At a time when India was experiencing some of its worst famines ever, an outbreak of Bubonic Plague started in Bombay. Probably carried by rats from ships which had come from the Far East, the epidemic eventually spread to Cawnpore.

In fear and ignorance of a disease which was highly contagious and resulted in a swift and painful death, the Indians reacted badly to the less than tactful approach taken by the authorities in handling the outbreak.

Industry ground to a halt and rumours were rife. There was talk of the bodies of those who had died, (whether or not it was proven that the cause of death was bubonic plague), being seized from their family homes and burnt. Finally a frenzied mob ran riot, destroying the plague hospital, setting fire to huts and killing police and doctors. The Cawnpore Volunteers were called in to assist, but they were forced to defend themselves by firing rounds above the heads of the rioters who turned on them too. Mac and Georgina were probably in Scotland at this time and missed the excitement but, thanks to Mac's leadership, the troop would have been well prepared and ready and able to assist the police and the professional soldiers.

Georgina and Mac took the many opportunities afforded to socialise and enjoy a wide range of activities in their new life in India. Mac was to become involved with institutions and organisations where his knowledge and expertise were to prove most beneficial. The couple's commitment to helping people less fortunate than themselves also led to their involvement in numerous charitable activities, both locally and nationally: a foretaste of things to come.

CHAPTER 4

Missions of a Memsahib

Her kindness and goodness were so well known, but her duties were carried out completely without ostentatiousness or obtrusiveness.

This was how the Indian *Daily Telegraph* of Lucknow described Georgina's character when she died in 1905.

It does seem that she got on with whatever was required of her without any fuss and sought no recognition for her good works. Given this reticence, it is not surprising there is little in her diaries about them: instead, she seems to record mainly the minutiae and the trivia of her life and her unwavering love and concern for those at home in Scotland.

Georgina's days were busy and varied. She could be presenting prizes to the children at the American Episcopal Mission or dealing with the tribulations associated with the dusters. Although life in Cawnpore was a whirl of social activity, the couple, in common with others of their status, took an active part in improving the lives of those less fortunate, especially the Indians and Anglo Indians. They saw it as their duty.

Within days of her arrival in Cawnpore, she records a visit to the mill in her diary:

Thursday, 26 Nov – … Saw over the mill in the afternoon most interesting to see the looms at work and the wool being spun.

In those early days in Cawnpore, when she first took her place at Mac's side, the mill workers and the community at large could not have suspected how profound an effect this unassuming lady was to have on the wellbeing of so many. But the tributes paid to Georgina when she died were unstinting in their praise for her charitable deeds:

"She was universally loved and respected and will be sadly missed in a place where she has done so much good", said one. Another read: 'Her kindness and goodness were so well known, but her duties were carried out completely without ostentatiousness or obtrusiveness'.

Everyone agreed she was a modest woman but she was held in such great affection and esteem that she was dubbed the 'Mother of Cawnpore'. After her death, Mac ensured that her name remained alive through many philanthropic gestures in her memory.

Gradually, as people got to know Georgina and to recognise her worth, they sought her help with a variety of good causes. She was tireless in her charitable work in Cawnpore and further afield in India; her strong Christian faith undoubtedly inspired all that she did.

The industrial revolution and the expansion of the British Empire after the mid-1800s had caused women to leave their familiar surroundings and seek work in factories. In a bid to offer support, housing and education to the most vulnerable amongst them, the Young Women's Christian Association (YWCA) was inaugurated in 1875. The first local association of the organisation in India was formed in Bombay, and according to an obituary when she died, Georgina had served as a President of the Association, although it does not state whether locally or nationally. Its aim of bringing women and young girls together, regardless of caste, creed, race, nationality or social and economic status, through a variety of services, would have been dear to her heart.

At that time, Lord Dufferin was Viceroy of India. His consort, Hariot, made her mark as one of the most successful diplomatic wives of her generation, as Rudyard Kipling recognised in his poem *The Song of the Women*:

The consort of a ruler— more than human—
Remote, unseen, a gracious name alone?
Nay, surely, for we know her very woman
Who, stooping down, hath made our woe her own,
Fear not, O wind, but swiftly follow after,
And take our cry, half weeping and half laughter.

In 1885, the year of Georgina's arrival in Cawnpore, Lady Dufferin had set up a national association for supplying medical aid to the women of India. This was known as the Countess of Dufferin Fund.

At a time when there were few facilities for women in childbirth or who were ill, the Fund embarked on an initiative aimed at recruiting and training women doctors, midwives and nurses. It also set up hospitals throughout India in Lady Dufferin's name, including one in Cawnpore.

Such was the charisma and the enthusiasm of this remarkable woman that she inspired others to become actively involved in the initiative. Georgina was recruited when Lady La Touche, wife of the Lieutenant Governor of the United Provinces and a keen supporter of the Vicereine, sought her advice about how to attract more nurses to work there. Sir James La Touche sent a special train to convey her to the meeting. Georgina, the child of an Aberdeen tenement and manager of a laundry, had arrived: she was now a respected social reformer with the ear of the great and the good of the Empire.

Mac was busy too. The patronage of leading members of the business community was much sought-after by those attempting to improve the lives of those living in poverty. A few years before Mac's arrival in Cawnpore, Hugh Maxwell, a pioneer of industry in Northern India and Gavin Jones' brother-in-law, had joined the committee of the Society for the Propagation of the Gospel. His roots also lay in Aberdeenshire where his grandfather had been minister of Newmachar Church. He enlisted Mac to help raise funds to rebuild an orphanage destroyed during the Mutiny.

Mac became an enthusiastic supporter of the SPG. The organisation had been founded in 1701 by the Anglican Church, and since 1820, its missionaries had been engaged in providing pastoral care and education to both the indigenous population of India and the colonists. They set up the Cawnpore Free School and preached from Christ Church.

In 1889, the Bishop of Calcutta intimated to the secretary of the Society in London that he was in need of additional volunteers to help in Cawnpore. By coincidence, on the same day, the secretary also received a letter from the Canon of Westminster, later the Bishop of Durham, indicating that his sons, George and Foss Westcott hoped to serve as missionaries in India. Thus, their wish was immediately granted and they sailed for India to find out, just as Mac had, that significant challenges lay in gaining an understanding of the culture, customs and beliefs of the people of post-Mutiny Cawnpore. Yet the Westcott brothers saw that the rift in the community needed to be healed and their first aim was to make education available to all. They also gathered a band of willing volunteers to help raise funds and care for the church and formed the St Andrew's Guild. Georgina joined this band of willing helpers – and also the choir. Mac was roped in to teach book keeping.

George Westcott put an ambitious development plan in place and soon, from its humble beginnings with just two classes, the school became a college. Its academic prowess was recognised in 1892 when it became affiliated to the University of Allahabad and was renamed Christ Church Collegiate School. This new status enabled George to secure the services of two Oxford graduates as teachers.

Foss's remit was to look after the mission boys. An experiment where difficult orphans had been sent to serve as apprentices in the Cawnpore Mills had ended in failure. The orphans were unsupervised outwith working hours and, since they were poorly housed, trouble followed. The mill owners wanted to wash their hands of them. Foss's answer was to take the boys to the mission, build living quarters for them and train them in their own workshops. One of the trades on offer was printing. They produced publications such as the Church magazine, directories and periodicals, as well as the weekly newspaper. Another was joinery: the boys were taught to make good quality furniture for which they were awarded a gold medal at an industrial exhibition in 1902. Many churches in India and Burma were adorned with the fine brass work that the boys produced in the foundry under the supervision of skilled British craftsmen.

George and Foss held many discussions with Mac and with William Cooper, primarily on labour relations and issues that arose about employment. Both Mac and William were radical thinkers who had positive views on India as a developing nation and Mac spoke of them to audiences throughout the world in his capacity as President of the Upper India Chamber of Commerce. Those views were not always the general consensus: there were some in Cawnpore who considered it a mistake to Christianise and educate these boys.

The girls in the orphanage were looked after by English missionaries and teachers until they were sixteen. The Christ Church School and Mission for Orphan Girls lay close to the mill and The Sheiling. This was very convenient for Georgina who took a keen interest in the work being undertaken there. Mac and Georgina were also enthusiastic supporters of the mission hospital. Its foundation stone was laid in 1898 and many of the girls from the orphanage went on to train as nurses there. The staff at that time comprised two doctors, two nursing sisters and an evangelist, all of whom were British. Matron was an Anglo Indian and about twelve Indian nurses were trained there. The mix of races working closely together to overcome the challenges of caste prejudice and the lack of knowledge of disease and hygiene issues was another step in bringing the community together.

'The coming of the Westcotts to Cawnpore transformed the whole character of the City,' wrote one enthusiastic commentator, but the MacRoberts also played their part.

George Westcott and Georgina had much in common, including their love of gardening. George created nine rose gardens laid out round a sundial. It was said his house was filled with the delicate fragrance from the cut flowers. The hard work by these missionaries, industrialists and energetic women continued to pay off: students won scholarships and achieved degrees; they learned to appreciate the arts; they were successful at sport and appreciated the benefits of having a library.

As the community flourished, so did the careers of the Westcott brothers. Years later, on the night Georgina died, Foss was ordained as Bishop of Chota Nagpur, a step on the ladder of an illustrious career. He became the Metropolitan of Calcutta and George the Bishop of Lucknow.

The MacRoberts also supported the children's home in Kalimpong, known from its inception in 1900 as St Andrew's Colonial Homes and from 1947 to this day as Dr Graham's Homes. This cause was so close to Georgina's heart that, after her death, Mac erected a clock and chimes there in her memory.

John Graham, founder of the Homes, prepared for the Ministry at Edinburgh University and his enthusiasm and vitality brought him to the attention of those who could further his career in the Church.

Through his involvement with the Young Men's Guild of the Church of Scotland, John Graham was chosen to be the church's missionary in

Kalimpong, and went there with his new wife Katie in 1889. Katie's mother had been a favourite nurse of Joseph Lister when he was conducting his experiments in antiseptic surgery. Her parents both belonged to Moray in Scotland, west of Aberdeen.

In 1889, Kalimpong was a mere collection of huts sitting on a ridge in the Eastern Himalayas. The original aim of the mission was to encourage Nepal, Tibet, Sikkim and Bhutan, all Buddhist countries, to open their doors to Christian missionaries. As he travelled through the area, Graham discovered that mixed race children, who were often the results of liaisons between Scottish tea planters and local women, were shunned by both races. He decided to set up a community where the children could be cared for and educated. The Church of Scotland refused to fund the project, so Graham decided to raise the money from the merchant princes and business-men, particularly those with Scottish roots like Mac.

He told them that 'the burden of supporting and assisting this community unquestionably rests upon every man who has either made India his temporary home, or who has a stake in the country from which he derives a reserve.' This cunning piece of emotional blackmail soon had the desired effect and the money was raised.

Mac set up a local committee in support of the homes and became their Honorary Vice President. Later he helped fund the purchase of land so that they could expand to accommodate the increasing number of children in need of assistance. Dr Graham wanted the homes to be self-supporting. He had been brought up on a farm and decided to set one up to provide funds. The children were encouraged to help.

Other enterprises grew up around the complex. The children were trained to work in the store and bakery and in the clothing department where their uniforms were made. The boys learned to repair and maintain machinery in the workshop. The girls took first aid courses at the medical centre and some of them went on to train as nurses.

Georgina was keenly interested in this charity and did much to advocate its cause in Cawnpore.

Each cottage within the complex was named after a sponsor and the aim was for the children to experience life as it would be in a family home.

44

MISSIONS OF A MEMSAHIB

From a small group of six in 1900, the population of the home grew rapidly as news of its success spread, and in 1902 there were seventy-two children living there.

But there was soon another call on Georgina's kindness and on the peace-keeping skills she had so quickly learned in Cawnpore. A tense situation had arisen between Mac and his father. Acrimonious and inflammatory letters flew between India and Scotland. If Douneside, their pied à terre, was to remain in the MacRobert family, she had work to do.

CHAPTER 5

Farms, Families and Feuds

The small estate of Douneside – held as a single farm containing 115 acres arable and seven acres of fir wood and hardwood belts. It is favourably situated within one mile of the village of Tarland, with a sheltered and sunny aspect to the South and South East and commands a pretty view of the valley of Cromar and the Deeside hills beyond. The dwelling house is rather a superior double cottage with back kitchen wing, with out houses well finished and surrounded by a moderate sized and well stocked garden. The possession would have considerable attractions to a retired person fond of farming and country life. There is a good dwelling house and the place is near the village for supplies and where church, school, market, doctor and bank is available.

By 1888, the Cawnpore Woollen Mill, which only four years earlier had been teetering on the brink of bankruptcy, had become a thriving enterprise. Its 2,000 employees were now so skilled and efficient that the services of Cooper Allen, the managing agents who had hired Mac, were no longer required. The New Egerton Woollen Mill was also flourishing and with contracts secured, Mac was reaping the rewards of his labours and of his canny purchases of shares in the Mill when they were going cheaply.

With Georgina's encouragement – she always missed the old country – he decided to use his profits to buy a farm in Aberdeenshire: it would provide them with somewhere to stay during their trips home from India and might also prove to be a shrewd investment. The agent he hired in Aberdeen presented him with the Land Valuator's report quoted above. And so Mac and Georgina found Douneside, a place where the MacRobert name still lives on.

Mac's love of the land may well have been bred in him. His maternal grandparents farmed at Banchory Devenick on the outskirts of Aberdeen, and as we have seen, his father, John McRobert, was at one time employed as a dairyman. In 1873, he emigrated to Canada with Mac's mother Helen, their son Johnny and their daughters, to try his hand at farming.

In 1880, following an unsuccessful application for a new job, Mac had visited Canada where he was reassured to find the whole family busy on the farm at Hopeville, New Brunswick. They had cleared the land, built a house and erected farm buildings. Although he was not tempted to join them, the observations that he jotted in his notebooks reveal his interest in agriculture:

> Fences around fields. No nails used … Oxen two wheeled cart with hay … Pigs go in the fields … Device to prevent cattle, pigs and horses leaping fences.

Over the next few years, the McRoberts succeeded in adding to their acres by buying an additional farm. They seem to have farmed well, since they enjoyed some success on the show circuit where their cattle won prizes. But as time went on, their letters became less enthusiastic about life across the ocean.

Mac who was never one to miss an opportunity, may have been inspired to search for a farm by John and Helen's plight. One of his ambitions had long been to create a 'model farm'. If he could persuade them to move back to Scotland he would have the comfort of knowing that his family was overseeing the work needed to make his dream come true. John, Helen and Johnny took up the offer: it meant they could return to a home and a means of earning a living. Georgina wrote to them:

> I do like to see people who have worked hard enjoy a quiet evening of life' … you must have worked hard and sore at Hopeville what with clearing the ground etc. and had little return for all the toil expended.

The letters suggest that the McRoberts senior were still in Hopeville when Mac completed the deal to buy Douneside. He exhorted his father to sell the farms, lock, stock and barrel but not to throw them away:

> It will be as well if you can wind up your affairs … as quickly as possible as I doubt if Douneside is now in good hands and it would be a pity to let it get into bad order.

Mac probably intended to make his parents tenants at Douneside. They would pay rent and manage the grieve and the two or three workers needed to run the place. Until a reasonable rent could be negotiated, John and Helen were expected to contribute to the mortgage payments. They would also be responsible for seeing that Mac's plans for the farm were carried out. Under those circumstances, Georgina's desire to see his parents have a 'quiet evening of life', as she put it, may have been difficult to achieve.

Midway through the century, Robert Peel's government advanced a loan of £500,000 to improve drainage in Scotland and the records show that no county took greater advantage of this opportunity than Aberdeenshire. Its landlords and tenants spent large sums of money and expended much energy improving the drainage of wasteland, mosses and bogs. Mac and his businesses in India provided the working capital for these and other improvements to the farm.

At this distance, it is difficult to know what sparked the conflict between Mac and his father. The whole affair seems to be out of character for them both, yet the situation went from bad to worse. In fact, the men were at loggerheads from the very beginning of the tenancy. One fly in the family ointment was the behaviour of the agent who had been hired to find and acquire the farm.

When he had succeeded in buying Douneside he also, as was common practice, purchased many of the implements at the ensuing roup. Mac was disappointed though that he had let a fine herd of Aberdeen Angus cattle slip through his fingers to another bidder. And there were rumours that his affairs were not all that they should be.

In a letter written at some point after the deal had gone through, but before John and Helen's arrival at Douneside, Georgina noted:

> It will be a great relief to Mac to have you safe and sound as you see from
> the accounts I have sent you how extravagantly they have gone in for
> bedding, harness etc.

It turned out that the agent had bought equipment that was not needed and that he had got into debt as a result. This was not Mac's way of going about things. Whether it was because he found it difficult as an absentee landlord to place his trust in others or whether it was his abhorrence of waste, the parsimonious Mac only seemed to be willing to spend if he could be certain of getting value for money. Perhaps this was the secret of his success in business. Setting up a farm was a costly affair and he would have questioned whether the agent's expenditure was justified or if he was being extravagant.

At the back of his mind would have been the gossip-mongers' whispers that the 'agent's affairs were rather involved', and that may be why Mac insisted that his father should check that all the accounts had been paid and verified by stamped receipts.

Letters took six or seven weeks to reach Cawnpore, and Mac and Georgina were impatient to hear what the McRobert seniors thought of Douneside. The Land Valuator's report was enthusiastic, if a little understated. The farm, it said, commanded a 'pretty view of the valley'. In fact, Douneside to this day enjoys one of the most beautiful views imaginable across the Howe of Cromar to the hills on the south side of the River Dee. Dramatic Lochnagar, a favourite hill of both Queen Victoria and the poet Byron, and Mount Keen, the most easterly Munro, both stand sentinel on the far side of the valley. Douneside nestles on its northern flank in the shelter of the hills of Pressendye and Pittenderrich.

Valued at £2,500, the land was generally of reasonable quality and enclosed by well-maintained stone dykes. Only a small portion was deemed 'light' and just a few acres classed as poor and rocky. The fields were serviced by running water and the stream flowed strongly enough to power a threshing mill.

Helen would probably have appreciated the 'rather superior' double cottage and the 'well fenced productive garden' and there was an extensive range of well-maintained outhouses that could be put to good use.

Although Mac's motives were understandable, his curt questioning of his mother virtually amounted to an interrogation:

What are the belts of trees like? Thriving?'
Is there a mill dam? If so is it suitable?

His orders too, were peremptory:

Let me have a full report about the state of all the buildings and if these are worth putting into proper order. Describe them fully please.

> Get the house comfortably furnished at your convenience, tidy up the
> garden and make the whole establishment a model.

John and Helen had arrived at Douneside to find an indolent workforce who
had taken advantage of the absence of a 'master'. For people of advancing
years, licking the staff into shape and working alien ground with little
knowledge of the crops indigenous to the area must have seemed onerous
tasks. The letters reflect rising frustration and bitterness on both sides.

The dictatorial tone that Mac adopted in a letter written from Cawnpore
on 1 September 1888 must have riled the old man:

> You do not seem to realise that you are the *master* at the farm, and that
> what you say is law. We do not see why the men should make a bothy
> of your kitchen. Have them sent at once to the croft house.

> You are altogether mistaken in supposing that I wish Mr ... to manage
> or act as factor for the estate, and I am surprised you should have
> imagined such an idea could enter into my head. Now that you are in
> possession, and in charge, Mr ... has no authority to do a single thing,
> and he understands that quite well. I wish you to act upon this distinct
> understanding.

The agent did not seem to acknowledge that John was Mac's representative,
and so made little effort to discuss farm affairs with him. Instead he acted
independently and shortly after their arrival on the farm, even stopped
communicating with Mac in India.

The situation deteriorated further when Mac wrote to his mother:

> If anything has been done that should not have been done since you
> arrived, I shall hold father entirely responsible.

John recognised the agent's failings and expressed his concerns in his letters
to Mac. Despite this, Mac did not seem to want to tackle the problems,
preferring instead to leave his father to deal with the situation. Running all
through these letters, and in his correspondence with Johnny after their
father's death, is more than a hint that Mac thought that the people at
Douneside were exaggerating the situation. However, he came to regret not
dealing personally with the agent.

Things got even worse when Georgina wrote insisting that the farm had to be profitable. Mac, she reminded her mother-in-law, had 'put all he has into Douneside and is in debt to the bank for a considerable sum!'

And Mac's grumpy behaviour towards his father will have added fuel to the fire:

> For the present I expect I must be content if you can make enough or spare enough to pay the mortgage interest and public burdens.

Although Georgina and Helen tried to keep the peace between the two, the exchanges between father and son became increasingly sour, with each blaming the other. Matters deteriorated even further when Mac insisted that his father should not get involved with the finances of the farm, despite the fact that he was responsible for its day-to-day running. Instead he was to send all the accounts he received from the agent direct to him in India.

Mac wrote to his father,

> Please do not make it necessary for me to write in this way again, you are giving yourself needless bother and annoying me at the same time.

Is it little wonder that John eventually stopped raising his concerns with Mac? Yet Mac soon realized that his father's fears were justified.

The agent confessed that he was in serious financial difficulty. It is likely that he defrauded Mac in some way, for Mac decided to prosecute him. The outcome however, is not recorded: at this point all correspondence on the matter comes to an end.

The couple's much longed-for first visit to Douneside came in 1890. It was not a success. John had a grievance which 'embittered my whole visit', according to Mac. It transpired that Mac had instructed his solicitors to draw up a lease that would also give John the power of attorney. John seems not to have understood the legal jargon and so viewed the whole proceedings with deep suspicion. He complained that he did not know what was expected of him, while Mac's frustration at his father's attitude nearly drove him to sell the farm.

Mac concentrated on making sure that his mother was comfortable in the house. During his visit, he ordered floor coverings to be sent to Douneside and in typical fashion, issued minute instructions as to where and how they were to be laid:

> In fixing the linoleum, use as few tacks as possible … You should at any rate get the male members of the household to cover the sitting room floor and the lobbies, if they are frightened, the dining room may await our return. …

And the letter went on in this vein.

On his return to India, Mac received a letter from his father that appears to have put paid to any hope that their relationship would ever be cordial again. He chose to reply to his mother:

> I have received from my father a letter – dated 13 October – the like of which I suppose was never written by a human being. It is the production of a madman or worse, and if it is the style he wishes to adopt towards me it will be far better to stop all communications. … I have had quite enough worry already about Douneside and I will not submit to any more. My father has chosen deliberately and wilfully to misrepresent and misunderstand my actions. … God knows I have done my best to make you both comfortable and have spent nearly one thousand pounds (in addition to the purchase price of Douneside) with that end in view, and it is hard to receive in return the blackest ingratitude. … I have quite enough work here, and if I am subjected to any more vexation about Douneside, I will instruct Messrs Collie to sell the place at what it will bring, and endeavour to forget that I was ever such a fool as to expect that what was intended for unselfish kindness would be appreciated, or that I would get credit for wishing to do good and not evil.'

He ends with a PS:

> Would it satisfy my father if we were to make a present to him of Douneside as it stands? He has already had gifted to him the greater part of the stocking and furnishings and cropping.

But his father continued to write, and a year later John still seemed to bear a grudge.

Mac responded:

> Until you can frankly get rid of the idea that seems to possess you that I am a swindler whose every action has to be carefully watched and counteracted, there is little chance of our having anything pleasant to say to each other.

In 1891, Mac suggested that, if his father wished to do so, he could leave on any terms he chose. The property would then be put on the market, since he had no desire whatsoever to see the place again. His dream of owning a farm that would give him some 'lively satisfaction' had been blighted by constant worries:

> I have quite enough to do with my work in India without being constantly vexed and annoyed from home. I hope you will see your way to come to a friendly understanding with me.

But John just could not let go and wrote again and again with his grievances. One dispute was over how much rent he should pay: £80 had been mentioned. It would appear that Mac was still footing the bill for the capital expenditure and that he sent a cheque in compensation for a bad harvest.

Despite all the family rows, when Mac and Georgina visited Douneside in 1901 during the 'season of mists and mellow fruitfulness', they realized they had found their rural idyll. They enjoyed playing golf on the lawn and feeding the calves. They watched the reaper cutting the oats and barley; the garden was producing fruit in abundance; the house was full of the scents of mint and honeysuckle. At last the improvements of the past few years had begun to pay off.

Little more seems to be recorded about Douneside from then until Georgina's death in 1905.

Did Mac and John make their peace in the intervening years? We have no answer to this question but the threat to sell did not materialise. Douneside continued to be farmed by the McRobert family and as time went by, the original 122 acre estate encompassed many thousands more. Mac's outlay of £2,500 proved, as he had hoped, a sound investment.

In 1902, the trials and tribulations of life back home in Aberdeenshire could be set aside. In Delhi, a Durbar had been proclaimed to celebrate the coronation of Edward VII, India's new Emperor. And Mac and Georgina had an invitation.

CHAPTER 6

The Delhi Durbar

How changed our life is. No thought of India then.

The Delhi Durbar, held over the two weeks that spanned the end of December 1902 and January 1903, is now regarded as the greatest spectacle in the history of Imperial India. According to one account, 'neither the earlier Delhi Durbar of 1877, nor the later Durbar held there in 1911, could match the pageantry of Lord Curzon's 1903 festivities'.

For them not to be at home in Cawnpore on the last day of the year was quite a departure for Mac and Georgina. Until then, they had always given their annual Hogmanay Party at the Lalimli Club. Georgina wrote in her diary on the 31 December that it was the first year since coming to India that they had gone to bed without seeing in the New Year. It was also their 19th wedding anniversary, and the rather endearing entry in her diary quoted above is proof of their continuing devotion to each other.

Their presence at the Durbar was testament to the esteem in which they were held. Officially, Mac was invited as the representative of the Chamber of Commerce's Legislative Council for the United Provinces of Agra and Oudh, but he had also earned his place at the magnificent celebrations for his contribution to the economic prosperity of Cawnpore and Imperial India. And Georgina, whose concern for the welfare of the mill workers had ensured their loyalty to the company, had also played her part.

Her excitement and enthusiasm leap out of the pages of her diary. She and Mac were mingling in illustrious company, the elite of the Empire, and occasionally she seems almost overwhelmed by the magnitude of the event, the hustle and bustle of the crowds and the demanding programme of visits laid on for their enjoyment. She appreciates Mac's encouraging comments on a dress he thought particularly fetching and on how gracefully she performed her curtsies.

The Durbar, which epitomised all the pomp, circumstance and pageantry of British ceremonial, was organised by the charismatic 'Viceroy of genius' Lord Curzon. As Viceroy, he was the Monarch's representative and India's own princes were subject to him.

The task was monumental but Curzon won through thanks to his meticulous attention to detail, his understanding of the complexities of protocol and his sensitivity to India's multifarious cultures. A master of logistics, he ensured that the tented camps and arenas were set up on schedule and that every need of the distinguished guests was fulfilled.

An added complication was that unlike the previous Durbar of 1877, this one was open to the general public. The Indian Army was ordered to add crowd control to its many ceremonial duties and the police were issued with uniforms specially designed for the occasion to make them readily identifiable. A magistrates' court was set up on site and stringent security measures were put in place to protect the VIPs. Roads and even a railway line were constructed and telephone and telegraph facilities set up.

The Durbar was held at the Ridge some seven miles from Delhi and Mac and Georgina arrived there on a train which Sir James and Lady La Touche had chartered for their guests. They found that much thought had been given to the needs of those who were to stay in the tented villages: sanitation, electricity and drainage had been installed; medical facilities were at hand; gardens were laid out to make the site more attractive.

The interiors of the tents, which were sumptuously lined and sported electric light, were said to resemble those of English country houses. Guests could relax on comfortable seats in front of fires and Georgina was charmed with the beautiful drawing rooms where even pianos had been provided for their enjoyment.

The cost of staging this spectacular event was said to be in the region of £180,000, the equivalent of about £10,000,000 today, at a time when floods and famine were causing great hardship in the country. A New York newspaper report said of Lord Curzon, 'The people asked for bread and he gave them a Durbar'. However, he contributed £3,000 of his own money to the cost and the creature comforts of the guests were funded by the Chief Rulers and Government representatives. The event attracted world-wide media coverage, and just as they are for today's major occasions, souvenir books were published and commemorative medals produced.

Curzon was passionate about India's heritage. He worked incessantly to protect and preserve its culture and monuments and he seized this opportunity to use the celebrations as a marketing tool to promote India. He may also have hoped to appease his critics and justify the expenditure by having a building specially erected to house an exhibition of the Arts of India. At the Gardens of Kudsia, a few miles from the main camps and linked by a railway, he gathered together a magnificent display of the skills of India's craftsmen which he hoped would encourage world trade and instil pride in the hearts of the people. Ironically, in his opening speech Curzon warned of the threat of cheap imports from Britain. He certainly seems to have been eager to persuade the guests at the Durbar to part with their cash, and after two weeks of being wined, dined and feted, they seem to have been happy to comply.

Mac certainly did. A cashmere carpet that Georgina particularly coveted found its way back to The Sheiling. The Lalimli trademark was represented at the exhibition and Mac visited the display tent to check that all was well.

The celebrations were more than a trade fair, however: Curzon had planned a spectacular demonstration of pomp and circumstance. So he was all the more disappointed that King Edward did not attend the Durbar himself but sent his brother, the Duke of Connaught as his representative.

Despite this, the Proclamation ceremony was a triumph, bringing together in a kaleidoscope of colour those who during the course of India's sometimes turbulent and violent history, had been sworn adversaries.

Of the 103 Chief Rulers invited, 100 were present. The Princes of India, bejewelled and bedecked with priceless gems, vied with the members of the British contingent who had been advised that protocol demanded they display their own most opulent jewellery. Sapphires, emeralds, rubies and diamonds flashed and sparked in the sunlight. Even the elephants seemed to be competing with each other for the most ornately-dressed title.

Georgina records:

The elephants were a fine show, but to my mind passed too closely together. One could not see all the beauty of their trappings and one of them had a chandelier on his trunk, another carried a chowrie and saluted with it as he passed the colours.

Gold and silver, crimson and turquoise, — the arena was ablaze with a riot of colour. In that magnificent setting, where the men of the Gordon Highlanders stood to the fore, Mac and Georgina, who were seated in the south stand, could see representatives from foreign states including South Africa, Australia, Japan, Afghanistan and Persia. Indian culture demanded that the wives and female relations of the Princes should be hidden from the public gaze: they viewed the proceedings from a curtained box. There were judges in full regalia; military men proudly sporting splendid uniforms sat alongside civil servants and Maharajahs. All had come together to proclaim Edward King and Emperor.

The event got underway with the arrival of The Viceroy and Vicereine and the Duke and Duchess of Connaught. Georgina noted in her diary that 'He looked like a gentleman, but she seemed sulky and not at ease in her chair and when the Viceroy came with Lady Curzon and sat by her, she did not smile and respond.'

Georgina was right. There was an atmosphere between the two couples. In her message to the Durbar of 1877 Queen Victoria had supported the British Government's hope that the principles of liberty, equity and justice would prevail in Imperial India. She wished to promote the happiness of her subjects, to add to their prosperity and improve their living conditions. This was a view also held by Mac and Georgina, who, as we have seen, worked hard to better the lot of their workers. But many thought differently.

In 1903, there was still widespread prejudice against the Native Indians, especially amongst some troopers from the 9th Lancers. Yet they, at the request of the Duke of Connaught, escorted him and the Duchess into the arena. This was despite the fact, or maybe because of it, that Lord Curzon had recently had reason to chastise and discipline members of the regiment for their treatment of natives whilst off duty.

Curzon wrote:

As I sat alone and unmoved on my horse, I could not help being struck by the irony of the situation. There rode before me a long line of men in whose ranks were most certainly two murderers.

Curzon felt the Lancers did not deserve the honour: they had brought disgrace upon themselves and acted against the principles expressed by Queen Victoria. The soldiers of the 9th Lancers were recruited from the well-connected elite, and Curzon's decision to make an example of them was unpopular in High Society back in England: hence the Duchess's disapproval which Georgina had detected. The crowd too, chose to express its displeasure at the Viceroy's stance by rising to their feet and cheering in support of the Lancers.

Curzon was also criticised for risking reopening old wounds by inviting veterans of the Mutiny to take part in the parade, but this as it turned out was the most memorable part of the proceedings.

Georgina's account in her diary and Curzon's in his notebook, later published as A Viceroy's India, paint a truly poignant picture.

27,000 people waited in the arena as 40,000 troops and the bands of the twelve regiments that had fought in the Mutiny were assembled outside. At the sound of the bugle the crowd fell silent. Then, to the strains of See The Conquering Hero Comes, hundreds of veterans who had fought in the Mutiny marched in. Most of them were Indians. Some were supported by younger officers; others were dressed in shabby uniforms or civilian attire. All of them wore their campaign medals as proudly as the Indian Princes showed off their jewels.

'We all cheered and shouted till we were hoarse,' wrote Georgina. 'I could not keep back the tears, some of the veterans were so old and bent and scarcely able to walk.'

Curzon watched as one old blind soldier responded to the cheers of the crowd by turning 'his sightless orbs towards the cheering and feebly saluted. It was his last salute, for the excitement was too much for him, and on the morrow he died.'

He went on to note that the occasion was so moving that, 'as the band played Auld Lang Syne, there was audible sobbing both of men and women, and many in that vast audience broke down.'

Heralds delivered fanfares before each proclamation and those who made speeches that day spoke of hope, optimism, patriotism and loyalty.

That wonderful day, on which the King was proclaimed Emperor of India, set the tone for those that followed. Mac accompanied Georgina who was a devout Christian to a church service held on the polo ground. This was the only area large enough to accommodate the congregation of 15,000, which included several thousand troops. The 500 voice male choir sang from a stand about 300 yards away through megaphones.

Here Curzon's sense of humour and meticulous attention to detail stood him in good stead. He had asked Lord Kitchener, his Commander in Chief, if he would choose a hymn that he thought the troops might sing with gusto and enthusiasm.

Kitchener's immediate reply was 'Onward Christian Soldiers'. But when Curzon went through the verses with his customary fine-toothed comb he came upon the words:

Crowns and thrones may perish
Kingdoms rise and wane.

His reaction was swift:

This couplet depicts not merely a familiar contingency, but also a truth of abundant historical justification. But, as a note of rejoicing at the coronation of a monarch in the presence of his near relatives, it might have been thought inappropriate if not disrespectful and I was doubtful how it would be regarded by King Edward when he heard of it. So I passed my pencil through the Commander in Chief's choice and selected some more innocent strophe.

There were countless other events for the edification of the guests: fireworks, polo matches, military rides and displays. At a ceremony held to recognise the achievements of individuals, Mac and Georgina looked on proudly as their friend and business associate William Cooper of Cooper Allen was awarded a Knighthood in recognition of his services to India. Sensitive as ever to the nuances of protocol, Georgina noted that while Europeans received their honours from the Viceroy, the Indians were given theirs by the Foreign Secretary.

The Delhi Durbar was held at a time when the wealth and privilege of the British upper classes were at their zenith and this was particularly noticeable at the Coronation Ball. Though the jewels that adorned the guests were unique and priceless, every lady present was outshone by the Vicereine. Her necklace of diamonds and her tiara, on which each diamond point was tipped with a pearl, drew audible gasps of admiration when she made her entrance to the Ball on the arm of her husband. Her dress in cloth of gold was embroidered with tiny peacock feathers with an emerald in each 'eye'.

No wonder, as the glittering spectacle unfolded, Georgina wrote 'How changed our life is'. And for Mac, at least, it was to change still further.

CHAPTER 7

Levelling The Playing Field

The Englishman acts like an old time sailor; he manoeuvres in an unstable environment and he accepts that instability as a fact which he cannot change working in a highly competitive environment where the need is to act quickly and decisively.

If Mac ever heard these comments made by the French political commentator André Siegfried, he may well have uttered a wry chuckle.

With his businesses flourishing, his charitable activities proving satisfying and worthwhile and life on the domestic front ably managed by Georgina, Mac could now turn his attention to politics and reform. The economy was unstable and India was finding it hard to compete in world markets. Mac had learned that in India politics influenced not only business matters but also the judicial system and agricultural and social reform.

In 1880, before Mac came to India, the then Viceroy, Lord Ripon, had affirmed:

> It would always be the aim of the British Government in India to train the people over whom it rules more and more as time goes on to take an intelligent share in the administration of their own affairs.

Queen Victoria's proclamation of 1877 had started the process and Indians were increasingly employed as magistrates and civil judges and in clerical positions, although opportunities to join the civil service were still limited.

Sir Courtney Ilbert, a member of the Viceroy's council proposed an amendment to the law. The Ilbert Bill, as it became known, would allow Indian district magistrates and session judges jurisdiction over British subjects in the courts. Until that time, they had exercised the right to be tried by a European judge. The proposed amendment caused a furore amongst the British 'non officials', who were not asked for their views. They joined forces with the press, and after mounting a vigorous campaign to overturn it, they forced the government into agreeing a compromise.

This defeat for Lord Ripon and his officials was a turning point. Indian politicians had discovered that change could be brought about through organised campaigning: a lesson that was not lost on the Indian National Congress, first set up in 1885, when it began to advocate independence.

Lord Ripon seemed to be of the opinion that the Indians were exploited by employers who were only interested in lining their own pockets. Although there were some bad apples in the cart, most businessmen ploughed back substantial amounts of their profits into developing resources for the benefit of the Indians. They worked with the labour force and sought Indian investment to achieve this.

Ripon's attitude made it hard for businessmen like Mac. For example, when Mac became involved with the Government Boot Factory, he found that a contract awarded by one of the ministries in 1881 had set limits on the profit that could be made from the deal. The terms of this created a huge headache for Mac and jeopardised the viability of the business. He discovered that this culture of working to small profit margins had been nourished by rivals in Manchester, who feared what they saw as a threat to their export markets.

In later years, when Mac gave evidence to the Indian Industrial Commission, he defended industrial practices in India. He pointed out that although the English worker appeared to be between three and four times as efficient as his Indian counterpart, there were mitigating circumstances:

> The Lancashire operatives are paid according to the amount produced which must give them an incentive. Their machinery works faster. In India labour is so cheap they can afford to have many operatives. India aims to capture the domestic market and reduce imports.

Mac added:

> The quality of cotton produced in India can compete with any other produced in the world. Their special type of goods is in demand abroad and particularly sought after in China and Egypt.

Mac found another platform for his strong opinions about the future of his adopted country when he served as President of the Upper India

Chamber of Commerce from 1898–1908. Since the area had a population of 70 million, much more than the whole of Britain, he was in a good position to influence Government policy.

Between then and 1920, he attended five congresses of the Chamber of Commerce of the British Empire – in London, Montreal and Sydney. In 1910 he was awarded a Knighthood, an honour which went with the post.

Accompanied by Georgina, Mac attended the 1903–1904 Chamber of Commerce Congress in Montreal. The delegates toured boot and shoe factories and cotton, paper and woollen mills and debated the issues of the day. These included the defences of the Empire, the food supply of Great Britain, consular services, treaty rights, and the metric system and decimal currency.

Mac's speeches at this conference, and at the first conference of the India and Ceylon Chambers of Commerce which was held in Calcutta in 1905, tell us much about the conditions in the mills and those that prevailed in other Indian businesses. He also used these events as a platform to communicate his ideas on labour relations and to persuade other delegates to share his philosophy

He argued that India was being penalised for her enterprise and that trade relationships needed to be developed. He warned that industry, particularly cloth manufacturing, was now being hobbled by taxes and duties imposed by the British at the insistence of the Lancashire mill owners.

Mac's advocacy of free trade stemmed from the visits he had made to the House of Commons where he had heard Gladstone speak. He became a Liberal, and when in 1885 the Indian National Congress began to agitate for some form of independence, he argued that some small degree of self-government would allow the country to develop into a great manufacturing nation without hindrance from Britain.

In 1897, he acquired a vehicle to express the political views of the British business community by becoming the promoter and principal proprietor of India's only Liberal newspaper, the Indian *Daily Telegraph* which was published at Lucknow.

Mac's opinion was that Independence was inevitable, cooperation desirable and direction imperative. He was happy to use his influence and money to see this achieved. His friend George Allen of Cooper Allen and owner of the rival Pioneer newspaper begged to differ. It might be expected perhaps, of someone who was described by an adversary as being 'the worst type of educated Englishman, sneering at all things native and natives generally, always much guided by the opinions of a clique of civilians who were despots who wanted and want to keep the people forever in a cradle'. Allen was passionate in his belief that the government in India was 'founded on conquest and that India was so big, had so many languages, castes and customs' that it would be difficult for it to assume a national identity. His argument that the country was not ready to adopt western political ideas did not endear him to educated Indians.

From reading Mac's journals in which he kept records of the content of some of his speeches, it is clear that his great understanding of the people contributed largely to his success. This passage is typical:

> Non native proprietors of manufacturing businesses must understand the culture of the natives.
>
> Whilst one might presume that to offer a high wage would tempt the native – this is not the case.
>
> It is anathema for him to consider leaving his ancestral village and the associations of the environment he was born and brought up in and provided he has enough money to satisfy his simple lifestyle, he is content with his lot. He aspires to nothing else and the challenge is to encourage him to a better and secure lifestyle. Being cooped up inside is anathema to those used to work in the fields. Women bring their children with them when they are working in the mill – babies crawl about the floor.

He understood that high wages did not motivate his workforce and instead introduced some innovative incentives. Within their working day of 10½ hours workers were allowed four 15-minute breaks, with more in the hot season. A rate for overtime was agreed and women could have a day off every week, on a Sunday. Holiday pay was granted and a pension was paid to loyal workers when they became too infirm to work. This gesture was also made to relations of those who died or who were injured at work.

In around 1900, the scarcity of labour threatened the economic viability of the mills at both Cawnpore and Dhariwal. To avert a crisis, an 'introduce a friend' scheme was instigated. A bonus was paid to those who recruited new workers – but only after they had stayed for a month. The result was disappointing: only thirty-eight of Mac's 2,000 employees eventually qualified for this payment.

Along with the rewards of business success comes social responsibility and Mac, who had grown up in the culture of the enlightened Pirie of Stoneywood, was well aware of his obligations and of the importance of creating a loyal and 'harmonious' workforce in the atmosphere of distrust that prevailed after the Mutiny. Initially, these genuine attempts to improve the lives of his workers were viewed with suspicion, but Mac persisted.

One of his first acts was to set up model villages at Cawnpore and Dhariwal. These were laid out attractively. The houses were fireproofed and tiled and let out at a nominal rent. Though they were equipped with only the most basic facilities, such as drinking water and drainage, they were far superior to anything the native workers had lived in before. To these, after careful consultations, Mac added reading rooms and cooperative stores. New pharmacies and other medical facilities ensured that the inhabitants largely escaped the plague epidemics that devastated the region. Spurred on by these successes, Mac bought thirty more acres of land on which he built 500 homes.

Typically, he insisted that meticulous records should be kept of everything: the weather, European visitors, illnesses and births, deaths and marriages. On many a Sunday afternoon, Mac could be found sitting on the steps of the houses, helping his workers to understand their finances. Though he was genuinely interested in the welfare of the people who worked for him, there was an element of self-interest in all this: the loyalty shown by his grateful workers gave him a significant advantage over his competitors.

Mac also took a keen interest in agriculture. While farmers in Scotland were being encouraged to improve and reclaim their land and pioneer new farming methods, for their counterparts in India political indifference to their problems and the adverse weather conditions simply meant life or death. After the Mutiny, famines became endemic in India thanks to the policies implemented by the Raj. Farmland was converted to plantations, trading restrictions were imposed in the domestic market to boost exports and extreme weather conditions brought hardship.

According to one estimate, as many as 40,000,000 people may have died of hunger in the second half of the 19th century. Between 1897 and 1902, 4,500,000 people were on famine relief and the missions found themselves inundated with orphans and sickly children, many of whom later died from malnutrition.

Mac did what he could to improve the lot of the farmers and he was appointed a Governor of the Agricultural College in Cawnpore which opened in 1906. He urged the Indians to become less dependent on the industry:

> A large population of 300,000,000 depend on agriculture. The area under cultivation is so small that when the rains fail, famine stalks the land. For most, the concept of famine is difficult to comprehend. Normally even, only one meal a day can be achieved. In famine there is literally nothing. Rural areas suffer most. In the manufacturing cities of Bombay, Calcutta and Cawnpore there is no famine...
>
> It is important that the manufacturers and infant industries of India should be encouraged so that the country may be less at the mercy of the vicissitudes of the season than at present.

However, he could not escape tragedy in his own life: Georgina was ill with cancer.

CHAPTER 8

A Lasting Legacy

Her greatest influence was in the homes where trouble and sorrow had invaded and her ability to relieve and comfort her fellow men and women and help them from darkness to lightness was much appreciated.

Georgina and Mac had been apart for almost two years when she finally set out for India on the *SS City of Canterbury* on 22 October 1885. The long voyage from Liverpool to Bombay was the first of many tests that lay ahead.

She recorded in her diary that she felt 'utterly miserable' on the passage through the Bay of Biscay, although she did derive great comfort from the religious services held on deck on Sundays. She enjoyed the camaraderie between the passengers and celebrated her thirty-third birthday amongst them. She wrote that the Captain had a cake made and that they drank ginger ale and danced.

From the moment she landed in India in November 1885, she devoted her life to supporting Mac, yet she also made her own mark in her adopted homeland. The notebooks and diaries in which she recorded her thoughts speak little of the good works she did, but her concern and compassion for others, especially Mac's mother and his sister, come across loud and clear. In the many tributes paid to this modest Christian lady after her death, there was a common theme. She was, everyone agreed, 'a sweet womanly woman – a person who everyone turned to in times of trouble.'

So it was a devastating blow to Mac when the illness that she first mentioned in her diary in June 1901 turned out to be terminal. She wrote that her circulation was poor and that she was suffering from shooting pains, which she feared might come from a liver complaint.

By May 1904, she had undergone two operations and a year later she sailed from Bombay to Scotland where she consulted various doctors who decided that another operation was required. This was carried out on 1 July 1905, and she was so ill afterwards that she wondered if she would ever see her friends again. But by the 3rd of August, she was a little better and asked if she could go home to Douneside to be nursed by Mac's mother. Mac wrote home with instructions:

> She was very sensitive when well. I mean Georgina to have all the comfort and happiness this world can give her. She is the best friend I have ever had and she has been a good friend to you and to all my people.

He demanded that: 'Doors must not be allowed to slam, the dog must be taught that his place is on the floor, all movements must be silent – quietness and cheerfulness everywhere and all the time!'

Georgina's niece Annie was brought in to help look after her, along with a nurse.

Mac's diary entries, written from Douneside over the next few months, are harrowing to read. They record his efforts to relieve her pain and suffering during the last few weeks of her life.

His love and concern for Georgina shine through.

He wrote on 1 September 1905:

> She has two – six months to live and took it quite calmly. She didn't think it would come like this. She thought she would be an invalid wife needing tender care for indefinite years'.

15th September

> Slowly getting worse. Can't turn in bed without help. Says she feels well. Being carried outside daily.

Arranged for resting place in Allenvale Cemetery [in Aberdeen] and for the removal of her mother's remains to the same grave. Agreed that my body should rest beside her and this gave her great comfort. Recommended me to leave India and rest at home. 'Waterbed arrived.' This invention by Neil Arnott, in whose name Mac had given lectures at the Mechanic's Institute in Aberdeen, was to help alleviate Georgina's terrible suffering.

29 September

Has fallen off the past two days. It is torture to see how she suffers over the dressing of the wound.

4 October 1905

Wound started to bleed just as the nurse finished dressing. We were greatly alarmed. Dr arrived in twenty minutes. Thinks it is the end. Not sorry to go in that way. Can't speak above a whisper but quite cheerful.

10 October

Very very frail. Right leg become frightfully swollen. She is longing to be at peace. Amazing courage.

Dr thinks her a little better.

12th October

A sudden pain in her breast may be pleurisy.

A snowstorm on 13 October heralded a week of stormy weather. Her dressing, he noticed, was 'smelly', but she assured him that everything would be all right and that she was 'wonderfully comfortable.'

Dosing her with opium. She has been wondering who will close her eyes.

On 18 October, she confessed that she was very tired and could not keep up the fight. A week later, however, she was longing for her Cawnpore friends.

Several cheerful days followed, but then the pain she suffered when her dressing was changed was almost too much for her and she was in terrible pain from her swollen legs:

She feels the dark valley is being made very light for her. Her bitterness is truly past and she is ready to welcome us when our time comes.

By the second week in November, she wished that those who loved her would pray for her early release. She gave Mac her Bible, inscribing it 'To dear Alec from Georgina'. These were the last words she ever wrote. On 14 November he described how 'she broke down and clung to me like a fluttering, frightened bird might. She said she was afraid to go into the unknown but recovered her composure and slept like a baby.'

16 November

Worse. A robin came into her room.

23 November

Dr has never seen a wound like it. She is pitifully wasted.

Mac was in despair at Georgina's suffering. He recorded not only her pulse and temperature but also the effects of the drugs that were given to her. After she had been given a double dose of opium he noted that her mind was wandering but that she understood what was said to her.

Collapsed after dressing, hands blue, sent for Doctor.

On 30 November 1905, Georgina's courageous and harrowing battle came to an end. She died at 11.15 a.m. with the 'sweetest of smiles on her face and she looked young and beautiful,' Mac wrote. 'It was a heavenly smile.'

They dressed her in spotless white with violets at her bosom. Her funeral was held at Douneside on 4 December. Mac wrote:

Had the service at 10.00 a.m. at the house in the open air.

Her body was then taken by train to Holburn Street Station in Aberdeen where the large company of mourners, which included many Indian friends, gathered for her funeral at Allenvale Cemetery at 1.30 p.m. The coffin of polished oak was topped by 20 wreaths. Mac continued:

The Earl of Aberdeen, absent in London, sent his carriage to Allenvale. Much family and friends present.

Georgina was fifty-three.

To coincide with her funeral a memorial service was held in Cawnpore, where her Indian odyssey had begun twenty years before. As a mark of respect, the mill closed down for the day. When news of her death spread, tributes flowed in for 'Mother Georgie,' as she was affectionately known:

It would be hard to exaggerate her influence in the woollen mills.

The success of the mill was due in large measure to the untiring interest she took in the welfare and the comfort of the staff. The harmony there could be traced to her influence', wrote another admirer.

Took a keen interest in charitable and benevolent work.

She was one of those to whom the Upper India Nursing Association owes its inception.

A generous supporter of the local S.P.G. mission and of the Kalimpong Homes.

President of the Young Women's Christian Association for many years.

Actively interested in St Catherine's and Dufferin hospitals.

To know her was to love her.

And the Indian *Daily Telegraph* said of her:

> She was a lady whose kindness and goodness though so widely known and felt were chiefly characterised by the quiet and unobtrusive and unostentatious way in which her many benevolences were carried out.

Mac was overwhelmed by the obituary notices and by the letters of condolence. They were proof of the high regard and affection in which she was held. From all nationalities and creeds, ages and cultures, came stories of her dedication and compassion for others. He found them a source of great comfort. He made sure that the design of the granite memorial erected at her grave was appropriate and reflected their life in India.

The inscription reads:

In Loving Memory Of
Georgina Porter
For 22 years the Devoted Wife of
Alexander McRobert,
Woollen Manufacturer, Cawnpore, British India
Born at Aberdeen 11th November 1852
Died at Douneside, Tarland, 30th November 1905
For twenty years a resident of Cawnpore
Where her amiable and sympathetic character
and many works of benevolence and

Christian charity endeared her to a
multitude of friends of all degrees. She
loved the Lord her God and her neighbour also.
During a lingering and painful illness,
she maintained her fortitude and serenity
to the last.
Her body rests beneath.
My presence shall go with thee
and I will give thee rest.
EX.XXX111.14

Mac's own obituary, which appeared in the *Aberdeen Free Press* on 4 July 1922, acknowledged his devotion to her memory:

> His charities have been too numerous and often so unobtrusive for anything like a complete list to be given here. Much of his benevolence has been obviously inspired by the memory of his first wife, a lady greatly beloved by all who knew her for her natural charm and kindly character and by whose side he has been buried.

One beneficiary of Mac's philanthropy after Georgina's painful death was cancer research. This was then in its infancy, as an appeal issued by the British Empire Cancer Campaign at around the same time made clear:

> We are still ignorant both of the causation and cure of cancer. Many other diseases have yielded their secrets to patient investigation, and there is no reason to suppose that the problems of cancer will not eventually be solved. Yet thousands of suffering men and women, and those who suffer with them are asking how long they must wait, and if there is nothing that can be done to hasten a discovery which will bring relief to those whose outlook today is so hopeless.

Little more than a year after Georgina's death, Mac wrote to Professor Reid, Dean of the Faculty of Medicine at Aberdeen University, offering 'funds for the endowment of what might be called the Georgina McRobert Fellowship, founded by me in memory of my wife, for encouraging the investigation of the cause, prevention and treatment of cancer.'

Given his love and respect for Georgina, it is perhaps not surprising that his initial donation was £25,000, a handsome sum in those days, and the first of many.

His proposal, as ever, was carefully thought-out:

The income to be disbursed at the absolute discretion of the Medical Faculty of the University of Aberdeen by the appointment under such conditions as they may determine, of one or more holders of the fellowship and the payment of other necessary expenses in connection with the enquiry. In the event of an epoch making discovery in connection with the subject of cancer research the Medical Faculty of the University of Aberdeen to have the authority to allot all or any portion of the capital of the fund as a reward to the discoverer and also to the investigator or investigators whose work has in the unanimous opinion of the Medical Faculty contributed to the discovery. The Medical Faculty to be empowered at their discretion to associate with themselves any one or more men of eminent position in the medical world in order to assist them in coming to a decision in awarding any portion of the capital of the fund to the investigators or discoverers of outstanding merit.

In 1912, when Mac was conferred with an honorary degree of Doctor of Laws (L.L.D.) at a ceremony at the University of Aberdeen, his generosity was recalled in the citation:

The fellowship which he has founded in this University for the investiga-tion of the cause, prevention and treatment of cancer is a notable addition to the equipment of our medical school and a lasting testimony to his large hearted humanity.

In November 1915, Mac asked the Fellowship Committee to widen the scope of the Georgina McRobert Fellowship. It decided to set up a lecture-ship in Pathology with the emphasis on malignant disease at Aberdeen University. A year later Mac provided it with an annual income of around £750 a year from an endowment of shares. However, the post was not filled until 1920 when the First World War was over.

The job went to Dr John Cruikshank who had served with the Royal Army Medical Corps. He was eminently suitable: his peers described him as a man with 'brilliant ability and a very versatile mind'. Although malignant diseases were his first interest, his experiences during the war years had awakened an interest in bacteriology. He had been officer in charge of a mobile laboratory and advisor in pathology to the Third Army. Aberdeen University provided him with a laboratory and equipment, and Dr Cruickshank and his assistant Miss J. L. Lockhart made many important contributions to medical science.

Later Georgina McRobert Lecturers included W.G. Evans, a pioneer of radium therapy. One of his many significant achievements was the development of a radium 'bomb' which could deliver a dose of radiation 6 cm below the surface of the skin.

When Dr Evans relinquished the post in 1939, the funds available for the McRobert lectureship were transferred to pure research. This coordinated the work of the surgeon in charge of radium therapy at that time James Philip, and the radiologist in charge of the x ray department. Thus began an integrated approach to the management of malignant disease.

James Philip was a graduate of Aberdeen University and a skilled surgeon long before the advent of modern equipment and anaesthetics. During the Second World War, he undertook a large share of general surgery at ARI.

Radium was treated with great respect and care and the authorities were diligent in assessing the risk that might come from an air strike by the Luftwaffe on the radium held in the City. Consequently supplies were stored at Cove Quarry, on the outskirts of Aberdeen, in a concrete-encased safe at Torphins Hospital on Deeside, and even in huge Rubislaw quarry, which meant that a surgeon and a physicist had to climb down into the depths to retrieve each week's supply. In 1977, Dr Philip became the first Director of Roxburgh House, that superb facility which provides support specialist care in Aberdeen for patients with advanced cancer.

Dr Tarunendu Ghose followed Dr Philip. He was a noted researcher into the growth of tumours and co-author of an important paper which identified a direct correlation between the incidence of leukaemia and the doses of radiation received by the survivors of the atomic bomb explosions in Japan at the end of World War II.

When Mac died in 1922, he left £10,000 to ensure that the Georgina

McRobert Fellowship for Cancer Research endured, and perhaps in anticipation of the delay caused by Indian law in settling his estate, he stipulated that, until the principal sum could be handed over, £400 per annum was to be made available in the meantime.

While Mac gave his wholehearted support to Cancer Research in his native Aberdeen, he wanted Georgina's name to be remembered in the city that had been their adopted home. For many years, Cawnpore had lacked a hospital where Europeans could be treated, since the military and civilian hospital which served the community of 200,000 offered them few facilities. Mac may have remembered how Georgina had volunteered to nurse a stranger suffering from smallpox in her home at The Sheiling, and perhaps this is what inspired him to build a hospital in her name.

Its foundation stone was laid on 18 March 1916 by Sir James Meston, Lieutenant Governor of the United Provinces and a native of Old Aberdeen. It opened in 1920. The hospital, for Europeans and those of mixed blood who lived in the 'European fashion', stood on nine acres of land which Mac had bought for the purpose. It was well equipped and staffed by two resident nurses. There was room for twelve patients. A separate unit was built to accommodate four patients with infectious diseases, enabling them to be nursed in isolation. Future plans included the building of a house for a resident physician. Mac formed a Board of Management to run it and set up an endowment to provide for the standing charges.

He had a bust of Georgina placed in the staff duty room, for he said, 'I believe that Cawnpore will be glad to think that the hospital is to be associated with the name of the gracious lady who was my wife, and whose memory is cherished by the friends she made during the twenty years she sojourned in Cawnpore.'

Mac also wished Georgina's name to be commemorated at Dr Graham's Homes in Kalimpong. The couple had supported the project since its beginnings and had helped Dr Graham build more accommodation and to acquire land to meet the increasing demand for places.

A letter in the MacRobert Trust archives gives an insight into the background to Mac's next generous gesture. Written by W. A. Gourlay from Government House, Calcutta on 12 December 1919, it reads:

Before I left England, I had a meeting with the London Committee of the Kalimpong Homes and Sir Charles C. McLeod presided... The suggestion is that we should have a detailed plan of a beautiful church drawn out – that we should endeavour at the present moment to raise money for the body of the church, leaving matters such as the Tower, the wings or Chancel and the decoration to be carried out as memorials or otherwise to people in the future.

McLeod and I were inclined to think that this would be a better plan than to present the Homes with a brand new church, all complete which would perhaps prove in a few years to be too small for the congregation. You might think over the matter and let me have a line as to your views so that I could have it before me when McLeod comes.

What happened next is told in a history of the Homes:

Mr McRobert decided to supply the Tower in connection with the school and to supply it with a clock and chimes. The memorial was to be a constant reminder of Mrs McRobert. It was to add dignity and beauty to the settlement as well as to be of the highest utility. The Homes is grateful to Mr McRobert for his magnificent gift and the honour he has done the Homes by allowing them to have this memorial of one so dear to him and so universally respected and beloved by all who knew her is fully appreciated.

The Georgina McRobert Memorial Tower was a landmark for miles around. Ornate and sixty feet high, it greatly enhanced the appearance of the school block. Mac went on to donate 18,000 rupees, about £8,000 today, to the Homes in 1916. He also set up the Georgina McRobert Trust Fund which gave fifty rupees per month to the SPG Mission and to Christ Church.

Thus, in Cawnpore and Aberdeen, Mac ensured that his beloved wife would never be forgotten.

CHAPTER 9

Change and Chance

But O the heavy change, now thou art gone,
Now thou art gone, and never must return!
From *Lycidas* by Milton

Georgina's death left a huge void in Mac's life. His letters home show how sorely he felt her loss and how difficult he found it to accept that she would never be at his side again.

When Mac mentioned a proposed visit to the Cawnpore Woollen Mill by the Princess of Wales, his mother Helen replied that Georgina would have been so pleased and proud to be presented to the Princess and that it was poignant to see the first photos from India without Georgina. Mac was sad that Georgina had not lived to meet the Princess. She had been so excited about it and had been planning what dresses she would wear for the occasion. 'People have commented at how she would have distinguished herself,' he wrote.

The Cawnpore flower show, which she had always enjoyed so much, took place just after her death. This was another painful reminder of her absence, as was every step her grieving husband took in her 'beloved' garden. Mac coped with her loss in the only way he knew, by immersing himself in work in India, by driving himself harder and harder and then spending the fruits of his labours back home in Scotland.

His brother Johnny, who now managed the farm, also corresponded regularly with Mac. Life there was hard. The letters he wrote that winter of Georgina's death tell of the severe weather at Douneside where the snowdrifts were ten feet high. In these unforgiving conditions the cattle failed to thrive and his own health was suffering too.

To cap it all, in April 1906, just as the weather was improving, Helen wrote that she had suffered an 'accident' and confessed in letters to Mac that she was a 'bit battered'. Her health continued to give cause for concern, and Mac came home to Douneside just before she died that July. Johnny was now his only link with the farm, since their father had also died two years before.

Times were changing for landowners and farmers. In the years before World War I, the rapid industrialisation of Britain did not always benefit all sectors of business. The nation's new social conscience meant that land was needed not only for housing and factories but also for new hospitals, schools and recreational areas. It left farmers and landowners with the burden of producing more from fewer acres in order to feed a hungry nation. In the meantime, agricultural workers were deserting the country-side for work in the cities and their 'dark satanic mills'.

Mac knew that the answer lay in greater mechanisation and improved farming techniques. He had long wanted to turn Douneside into a 'model farm', and now he followed the example of his neighbours in Aberdeenshire. Many of them were Liberal MPs intent on radical land reform, while others like Lord and Lady Aberdeen at the House of Cromar nearby were prominent members of the party.

Mac would have known JW Barclay who, in 1901 bought Glenbuchat, an estate in Strathdon just over the hill from Douneside. He had held the seat of Forfarshire for the Liberals for nineteen years until 1892 and had fought hard, but in vain, for Aberdeenshire to be included in the Crofters' Holdings (Scotland) Act of 1886. The Act laid out the criteria for defining crofting parishes and it also granted security of tenure to the crofters themselves.

When he took possession of the estate, Barclay had found it to be in an appallingly run down condition: many of the houses were unfit for human habitation and the farm buildings were in equally poor repair. He set about improving both and to make the estate economically viable. He not only drained and fenced the land and developed it for field sports, but he also began to pioneer new, more scientific methods of farming.

Barclay had been a tenant on another estate at Auchlossan, Lumphanan, which was also close to Douneside. It had been owned by the Farquharson family of Finzean since 1780. When Dr Robert Farquharson became laird in 1876, he carried on with a scheme of improvement begun by his father.

Dykes were dug, fences erected, drains laid and farm buildings renovated: thus the estate was transformed into a flourishing business. Farquharson also served as Liberal Member of Parliament for West Aberdeenshire, the constituency in which Douneside lies. He proved a popular MP and followed the party line by supporting tenant farmers over their landlords when disputes arose.

With Georgina seriously ill, Mac had decided to stay in Britain for the duration. He had been a Liberal since listening to Gladstone speak in Parliament when he was young and in 1905, when Dr Farquharson announced that he planned to retire at the forthcoming General Election, he decided to seek nomination as Prospective Parliamentary Candidate. He believed that his business experience and his active interest in organisations in India gave him the qualifications to become a good constituency MP and he also hoped he would attract a strong personal following.

To further his cause, Mac enlisted the help of the President of the West Aberdeenshire Liberal Association, Sir John Clark of Tillypronie. He was a neighbour and son of Queen Victoria's physician and trusted friend, Sir James Clark. Sir John was willing to back Mac's application, but he warned him that there were other strong candidates who also wanted the seat. So perhaps Mac was not surprised when his application was unsuccessful.

Mac went back to improving the farm albeit in a more modest manner than his neighbours had adopted for their estates. A new byre proved a great asset and local tradesmen were invited to tender for work on the house. Mr Duguid from Ballater, James Emslie from Tarland and a Mr Brebner all submitted quotations for joinery work. Slaters John Cumming and R. Wright and son of Aboyne quoted £75.00 for the roof.

Mac, like the Liberal Government of the time, was committed to reducing the poverty he found in North East Scotland. In a letter written on 28 September 1906, the Rev Skinner expressed his thanks to Mac for his contribution to the village's Poor Fund and for the 'gold' which was found in the collection ladle on a day when Mac was present at a service in the village church.

Mac may have found some consolation during this painful period of adjustment to life without Georgina in an invitation, as the representative of Allahabad University, to the quarter-centenary celebrations of the University of Aberdeen. These were held in September 1906. The completion of the extension to Marischal College, which made it the second largest granite structure in the world, coincided with the anniversary. King Edward VII and Queen Alexandra visited the city for the occasion.

The University's Chancellor was Lord Strathcona, a Scot who had emigrated to Canada where he had made a fortune with the Hudson Bay Company. He presided at a banquet held in a sumptuous tent specially designed for the occasion. The 2,500 guests who included another philanthropic industrialist, Andrew Carnegie, the recipient of an honorary degree, enjoyed a nine-course dinner served by 500 waiters. Later that night, a spectacular fireworks display rounded off the four days of celebrations.

Mac's despair at losing Georgina and his mother in consecutive years did not distract him from his work. The MacRobert archives contain notes of the meticulous research he conducted as he considered building several new factories. These also paint a vivid picture of Indian life in the late 19th and early 20th centuries. For example, on a tour of Madras and the south in 1908, which he undertook for the Factory Commission, Mac described the area as a 'fertile land and although the people seem quite well to do, some of the lower castes seem to live in abject poverty.'

All through his life, wherever he lived and travelled, Mac took note of the local agricultural practices. On this trip, though he observed that paddy fields were being developed and recorded how the cotton was picked and processed, he was most concerned about the primitive conditions endured by the workers. Of one mill he wrote:

> Managed wholly by natives and in existence for twenty years, its five hundred employees work from dawn to dusk with no artificial light.
>
> Long hours are worked with a half hour break permitted. As absenteeism is not tolerated, 90 per cent of workers attend regularly for work. Women work the night shift.
>
> One factory employs a twelve year old and although the manager has supplied latrines, the place is unspeakably filthy.

His tour also took him to other businesses such as a cigar factory and a railway workshop, which, he observed, seemed to be suffering from a shortage of skilled labour. He was particularly interested in how one of the mills was powered: water cascaded 300ft from a dam behind the mills and was then fed through turbines by a steel pipe.

Socially, Mac felt Georgina's loss keenly but he had friends in India with links to home. Lord Pentland, the Governor of Madras was married to Marjorie Gordon, daughter of Lord and Lady Aberdeen, his neighbours on Deeside. Letters in the archives show that they kept in touch.

A trip home in 1909 was to change the course of his life – and those of many others. On the ship, Mac met a young woman called Rachel Workman. She was returning with her parents from a trip to India where they had visited the big cities. Mac and Rachel were introduced to each other by a friend. On 14 July 1909, Rachel confided to her journal that she had 'met A. McR' and that they had 'said tender farewells'.

An unlikely alliance soon developed. Rachel was thirty years younger than Mac and quite unlike Georgina. She was born of unorthodox parents who came from privileged backgrounds in New England. Her father, William M. Hunter Workman was regarded as a gifted physician and surgeon. Fanny Bullock Workman, her mother, was the daughter of a former Governor of Massachusetts. Soon after they married, William gave up his medical practice so that he and his new wife could travel the world.

The couple were pioneer explorers of the Himalayas, and together they conquered many of the range's highest peaks and discovered glaciers and passes never before traversed. They ventured into Asia and on into the Indian subcontinent where they became pioneers of a new type of adventure tourism: mountain climbing. They discovered new peaks, drew maps and made scientific observations. They did the same in Europe, where they charted routes for cyclists, published their first travel book, and shared their discoveries and experiences by giving lectures to geography societies.

Fanny set a world altitude record for women when she scaled a Himalayan peak of 21,000 feet, while in 1903 William, who was also a fearless climber, reached 23,394 feet on another mountain: another record. In recognition of their intrepid feats of exploration a 19,450 feet mountain in the Himalayas was named Mount Bullock Workman by the Geological

Society of London. The Workmans themselves named two peaks in the Karakoram: one after Rachel and another after their son Siegfried who died of influenza when he was three.

At sea level, Fanny was no less formidable. She was the first American woman to lecture at the Sorbonne in Paris and the second to address the Royal Geographical Society despite the 'sex antagonism' she claimed she had met from male scientists and climbers. Rachel's father too held very decided opinions.

Rachel's parents moved from America to Dresden in Germany and continued to travel the world. Rachel went to school there and the city became the closest thing to home that she would know. Since they were often absent on their travels, William and Fanny then sent her to Cheltenham Ladies' College in England to continue her education. From there, she went on to study at the Royal Holloway College, which was to become part of the University of London. Royal Holloway was established by the philanthropist Thomas Holloway who used the fortune he had made developing patent medicines to provide university education for women. For one year, between 1907 and 1908 Rachel also studied at Edinburgh University before graduating in 1911 from London University with a 2nd class Honours degree in Geology, the year that she and Mac married. But that was not to be the end of her academic career. She continued her studies at Imperial College, London, where she published papers on the igneous petrology of Scotland and the glacial geomorphology of Sweden. In 1919 she was appointed a fellow of the Geological Society of London and became one of the first women to be admitted to what had been a male preserve.

In a letter to Mac, she showed she was well aware of why she had been accorded this honour:

I am very much amused at the first list of sixteen women admitted to the F.G.S. There are one or two notabilities, the others merely wives. It is obvious why they were admitted at this juncture. They are badly needing additional subscriptions so the female subscriber has a financial value if none other. Poor, downtrodden race!

All this was in tune with what Fanny had told her when she was seventeen: 'Make no man your idol for the best man must have faults and his faults will usually become yours thus adding to your own'. Rachel, like her mother, was a supporter of the Suffragette movement. In July 1910, she wrote to Mac from York where she was staying with her friend Marjory Cudworth, telling him that she was going to a garden party for the National Union of Women Workers and that 'the Suffragette organiser' from London was coming to lunch.

A year earlier, in the summer after she and Mac met, Mac invited Rachel and one of her women friends to visit Douneside before they embarked upon a geological tour of America. Romance was blossoming. Mac was also off to America soon after and the couple met up in Seattle. Then Mac sailed with GB Allen to Australia where both were due to attend the seventh British Empire Congress of Chambers of Commerce.

Rachel's studies took her all over Europe so their courtship had to be conducted over a long distance. But when they met in 1910 in Oberammergau to see the Passion Play, Mac presented Rachel with an emerald engagement ring and they made plans to marry the following year.

Mac soon found that Rachel could be difficult. He had been awarded a knighthood in the New Year's Honours List, but she refused an invitation to Buckingham Palace from the King, declaring in a defiant echo of her mother's dictum: 'I will bow to no man'.

The relationship was complicated from the start.Mac accused Rachel of expecting him to acquiesce to all her demands but she wished, she said, for no responsibilities for she was selfish in comparison to him and had no intention of giving up her geological holidays after their marriage. She bemoaned her 'inexplicable contrariness' and her quick tongue but begged him to let her go her own way: 'enforced idleness etc. irritates me beyond measure,' she wrote.

Her father was puzzled and confessed in a letter to his sister that he had no idea whether his daughter was in love with Mac or not:

'I don't blame her for getting all she can out of it. So far they seem to get along well together.' He recognises that Mac is a very wealthy, self-made man and suggests that she has been quite calculating in choosing a man who can keep her in style.

Rachel in her turn was critical of Mac for what she called his coldness and for his relaxed approach to the arrangements for the wedding. They eventually agreed on a Quaker service at the Meeting House in York as a compromise between his desire for a religious ceremony and hers for a civil one.

Rachel had long been friends with Marjory Cudworth and was regarded as part of the family. They held a dinner for her before the ceremony which took place on 7 July 1911. It was a few days later than planned because Rachel was still busy with her final BSc examinations and Mac had been invited to the Coronation of King George V. GB Allan and Margaret (Marjory) Cudworth signed the register as witnesses to the marriage and among the guests was Logie Watson, Mac's fellow Aberdonian and Stoneywood papermill colleague who now worked in India.

Rachel wore a pale blue satin dress with a silver and grey veil. Because she came from a well-known Massachusetts family, (her maternal grandfather had been a governor of that State and her uncle was President of the State Mutual Life Assurance Company) the wedding made news. Beneath the headline 'Miss Workman Weds', the *New York Times* proclaimed:

London 9 July – The marriage is just announced of Sir Alexander McRobert, Manager and Director of the Cawnpore Woollen Mills Company of Cawnpore, British India, and Miss Rachel Workman, daughter of Dr W.M. Hunter Workman, the noted explorer, and Mrs Fanny Bullock Workman, the mountain climber of Worcester, Mass. The marriage took place at York on 7 July. Sir Alexander McRobert received his Knighthood in 1910. Before going to Cawnpore in 1888, he was a lecturer at several noted colleges. He was President of the Upper India Chamber of Commerce for nine years.

Another newspaper added: 'The news of Miss Workman's marriage was not a surprise to her Worcester friends who had known for some time of the attachment between Miss Workman and Sir Alexander.'

Rachel wrote to tell her relations and close friends when they got engaged. One, Maria Ogilvie Gordon, wrote from Aberdeen on 8 May 1911, responded cautiously to the good news. 'Are you finding yourself fully in love with Sir Alexander?' she asked. 'His absence will have made you feel the want of his thoughtfulness always around you. But be very sure. It's a pity your parents cannot be home for the wedding but you knew that of course.'

The marriage does seem to have surprised Rachel's friends, many of whom seem to have been unaware of her relationship with Mac at all. One of them did write encouragingly to congratulate her for choosing a Scottish husband: 'The Scotch are a remarkable race and ... are especially reliable as husbands.' Though Mac himself could be disparaging about his country of birth. 'Scotland', he once declared, 'was an excellent place to be born in... and a desirable one to get out of'.

Rachel's parents had known for some time of her plans to marry Mac. In a letter written on 1 April, 1911, from a place called Lovers Retreat in Rawalpindi, her father suggests it as an ideal place for them to spend their honeymoon. The lure of the Himalayas, however, was stronger than the desire to attend his daughter's wedding, and he wrote again on 8 July 1911 wondering what her 'sentiments' were and how she viewed marriage. In later letters he suggested she should keep her maiden name and become known as Lady Rachel Workman McRobert. He also mentioned Mac's will and suggested that she should also make one. In another grumpy letter, he feels sorry for her going to live in such a small country and deplores Asquith's handling of the coal strike. In March 1912, perhaps because he, like Mac, was a man of property, he sent her a newspaper cutting about the disadvantages of an international marriage, adding:

> It is settled that American women who marry Englishmen will have to pay an inheritance tax to England on estates which are left them by American relatives.

But despite the tensions that had at first surrounded their marriage, a brave new world was opening for this unlikely couple.

CHAPTER 10

Trials and Tribulations

Take an extremely kindly and charmingly volcanic hostess, put her into a most comfy house in beautiful Scotch scenery, surround her with three bairns, an excellent manageress – secretary, a governess, all agreeably mixed and rolled into one, a much admired nurse...

This comment, written in the visitor's book at Douneside, is typical of the reactions of Rachel's guests to the idyllic rural retreat that Rachel worked hard to create.

She found herself settling into her new life at a time when, in the years surrounding the Great War, political and social changes swept Britain. Medical care for children and old age pensioners was introduced and Lloyd George imposed a tax on landlords and the rich to pay for it all. The National Insurance Act provided health and unemployment benefits for workers but mass strikes by transport workers, railwaymen, miners and seamen swept the country. Rachel wrote to Mac that, 'England seems in a dreadful state and it is all most alarming'. Mac was at work in India for most of the time, but unlike Georgina, she disliked 'that nasty land' and declined to live there with him.

Instead, she combined travelling in Europe and continuing with her career with adjusting to her new role as mistress of Douneside and managing the farm. She learned fast, although her father still cast doubt on her ability to run a household. In a letter to his sister, William Workman also questioned whether she was up to being the wife of a merchant prince, describing Mac as an old, quiet man who spoiled her and indulged her every whim but whose status in 'colonial, imperial, monarchical India' meant that Rachel would have to be at his side at important events.

One of these was another Durbar, held in Delhi in 1911 to proclaim George V King and Emperor. Mac used the occasion to reward his employees and colleagues at the Cawnpore Mill for the contribution they had made to the success of the business. He arranged to transport more than 1,000 members of the workforce and their families to the Durbar on a specially-commissioned train. He also had a special commemorative medal struck for every member of the party. It showed the King on one side and the mill and the business's trademark, the Lalimli tree, on the other.

Rachel dutifully went with him, but while Georgina had enthusiastically and sensitively recorded her experiences at the 1902 Durbar, her comments were more restrained, as might have been expected of someone who had made it a principle to 'bow to no man'. She described the event as 'a very tiring and varied fortnight – but it was all very wonderful'.

Perhaps her low-key reaction was also due to the fact that she did not attend the Durbar Day itself because she was unwell. Other guests had succumbed to the extremes of temperature in Delhi, suffering from chills and fevers, but it soon turned out that Rachel's indisposition had another cause. She was pregnant though she had not yet told her family or friends. Although she was to bear Mac three sons, pregnancy did not suit her. 'You are certainly doing your duty by the nation,' Mac reassured her in an eerie foretaste of things to come.

Alasdair was born on 11 July 1912, followed by Roderic on 8 May 1915, and Iain on 19 April 1917.

With Mac usually abroad in India, Rachel had to assume virtually sole responsibility for the children's upbringing. To begin with, his long absences and the changes she faced on becoming mistress of Douneside made her anxious. Her letters to Mac at that time reveal how much she wished for him to be at home with her and she pleaded with him to reduce the 'hateful' visits to India. Some discussion must have taken place since she asked him to consider GB. Allen's suggestion that 'young Lilley', Mac's nephew Arthur, could be groomed to take over some of his responsibilities.

She was soon to be more cheerful. In March 1913, she was clearly in a light-hearted mood when she wrote to Mac: she was happy in her marriage, she had produced a wonderful son, and she was still engaged in a satisfying career. But while coping with motherhood was one thing, managing the house, the estate and its farming operations was another.

The Great War had changed the attitude of the rank and file to their 'superiors' though lairds were still expected to provide a reasonable standard of living for their employees, and their ladies were required to see to the welfare of the poor, sick and needy.

Rachel found hiring domestic staff a headache, but she was very supportive of her female employees. She kept the girls informed of their new rights and was pleased with their reaction when she explained the provisions of the Insurance Act to them:

> They volunteered the information that they thought it an excellent scheme and liked the idea of putting aside some money each week for future emergencies. They showed quite the right and thrifty spirit.

There were lessons to be learned as well as given. When a worker had an accident, the MacRoberts discovered they did not have the right insurance and that they would have to pay out a couple of hundred pounds in compensation. Rachel wasted no time in instructing their solicitors to ensure that cover was put in place: in future all the servants would be insured against accident and that the policy would also cover casual labour who came in by the day.

In her letters, she expresses her concern for the ill and poor in the area, and by giving the wife of a sick employee ten shillings a week, she showed her benevolence as an employer. She kept her ear to the ground though, and noted that the recipient of her largesse was generally regarded as 'an awful slattern ... [who] spends everything at once.' She made quite sure a receipt was obtained in exchange for the money.

She seems to have held Mr Pratt, the chauffeur in some esteem. After checking with the famously frugal Mac – and perhaps overriding his objections – she paid £14 to replace Pratt's uniform which he had worn for more than five years. And when the grateful recipient was emboldened to tell her about the conditions chauffeurs had to endure when their employers were visiting friends, she was appalled. Rachel valued and rewarded loyalty and endeavour: when Pratt fell ill, she arranged for him to visit a doctor and then to stay in hospital.

Rachel was still involved in the Suffragette movement whose members were growing more militant by the day. In one of her letters to Mac she says that suffragettes were now throwing explosives. They were active in Aberdeen: in 1913 they set fire to a school, and a year later, they had invaded a church and disrupted a service.

'Girls have no sort of life under present social conditions and the wickedness of men at large,' was her justification for these acts of violence.

Attitudes between staff and employers were changing however. In 1938, in a reply to a letter from his mother, Alasdair appears to be outraged by the behaviour of her 'insubordinate' servants. They were, he insisted, paid to do as they were told and not to organise the household or to object to the habits of their employers.

Rachel had her own little idiosyncrasies, and despite her generosity to others, she did share Mac's frugal habits. When she travelled to London on the overnight sleeper train, she was said to picnic on sandwiches provided by the staff at Douneside. Meanwhile her accountant who went with her enjoyed dinner in the dining car. While she was in London she had vegetables sent down from Douneside.

Rachel liked to spend the 'season' in Tarland, the time when summer elided with autumn and the landed gentry decamped from the cities to their Scottish homes to shoot by day and socialise by night. She took an enthusiastic interest in the archaeological excavations of the Deeside Field Club. With its hut circles and standing stones the countryside around Douneside was steeped in history.

Despite her father's misgivings, Rachel was a warm and generous hostess and invitations to Douneside were much sought-after. The artist Charles Horsfall, famous for his portrait of Lord Kitchener in the National Gallery, was not the only guest who inscribed a lyrical description of the place in the visitors' book:

The letter quoted at the top of this chapter continues:

Much land, berry carpeted woods – flower perfumed gardens. Add ten thousands of roses, many colours as the rainbow, a rock garden with burn and lily covered pools, season with an overfed pony and gorgeous pedigree beasties, sprinkle fowls, turkeys, ducks and a couple of goats and serve with tomatoes, black and red gooseberries, cran and raspberries, decorate with oatcake and salad leaves and serve the whole during hot summer months near a cool fountain to weary Londoners and in especial to the always grateful CMH.

Over the years, friends from all over the world enjoyed Rachel's hospitality at shoots, sheep dog trials and Highland Games. Neighbours from the other 'big hooses' in the area and their guests came too: Fergusons from Corrachree, Leiths from Hopewell, Roydens from Tillypronie, Shaws from Blelack, Sempills and Forbes Sempills from Fintray, Vaughan Thomson of Craigmyle, Vaughan Lee of Kincardine. Brigadier-General Hamilton from Skene House, Gen Sir Richard Bannatine from Auchenhove, and Lt. Colonel and Mrs Lumsden from Sluie. The Bell Tawses from Colquich visited, as did Mary Garden, the famous singer who came over from Pitmurchie and David Mason an MP and supporter of the Suffragettes from the nearby Lodge at Tarland.

She took her duties to the estate seriously although her principles and inclinations made her a reluctant landowner. She once told Mac:

I should also remind you of my inherent dislike for land – my ideal is to have enough room for one's own use and pleasure without the bother of an encumbrance of tenants and the troubles they bring with them … it might mean the beginning of endless worry and bother.

But in a letter to Mac when he was thinking of buying the neighbouring Melgum estate in 1912 she showed that she understood the need to become involved in the business side of things:

What is the rent role, how much do the tenants pay for the shooting months, is it likely to bring in more monies? How quickly would the purchasing money be paid off from rents etc?'

And she also reminded him of the effect that new legislation could have on his investment:

It would be stupid to pay such a large sum and then have the land stolen bit by bit by the Government.

She also admitted that she could not easily abandon her principles:

But I am sad and apprehensive about Melgum. I do disapprove of landed property and all that it comes with is in the eye of the public and think it wrong for one person to own large masses of land and then more or less close it to the public by 'preserving' it.

I feel it myself when I want to go on the hill in shooting time and have to consider the possibility of getting shot by Mr ... or disturbing the birds rented by him. I should hate to feel we were among the same class that close up places like the valley up Glen Tanar. Did I ever tell you my attempt last autumn to get to the foot of Mount Keen and landing instead at the Coates front door? Now that sort of thing is insufferable. I think one wants enough ground to live and play and the right to keep that quite private.

However, the Melgum deal fell through. Undeterred, when the property again came on the market in 1918, Mac instructed Rachel to negotiate to buy it. This time he hoped that although she was averse to acquiring more land she might have a 'new line of vision'. He had good reason to think so: she had her own herd of Friesian cattle which she had set up to provide for the baby Alasdair, who had failed to thrive on the low-quality milk offered by other local farmers. But again the bid was unsuccessful.

Mac had been on the look-out for more property for some time. In a letter to Rachel, he had bemoaned the fact that Douneside would not be suitable for the needs of a growing family: extra nursery accommodation was required and so were larger servants' quarters. Rachel was keen to go after West Town, a neighbouring farm, and this was offered to Mac as part of a deal.

She wrote on 5 February 1913, 'It would be so nice to move the farm higher up, and annexe the farmhouse as bedroom accommodation for Douneside – we certainly need it with our large family.' After much negotiation, that deal fell through as did their attempt to buy the Glassel Estate near Torphins.

Instead, Mac and Rachel decided to extend Douneside. While the building work went on, Mac rented Carnousie House at Forglen near Turriff in north Aberdeenshire. Iain was born there in 1917, when his father was in London nursing his sick friend and colleague, GB Allen. Mac wrote 'I am concerned about G.B.A., He does not pick up as he ought, and he is taking a morbid view of his prospects'. On 24 April, Mac recorded that his old friend was sinking fast. He died a few months later in June of that year.

In May 1917, Mac bought Ranna, a farm near Douneside, for £2,350 and put it in trust for Alasdair. The following year, tired of being incarcerated in Tarland in the winter and 'buried' there in the summer, Rachel bought a farm in England, Colney Park near St Albans. It was only thirty minutes from St Pancras station in London and next to one of the best preparatory schools in England. She thought it would be a useful base for the boys as she introduced them to the cultural delights of the capital and for her business and professional activities.

She wrote to Mac about the deal and her letter makes it clear that, although she was now a wife and mother, she was still determined to continue with her career and to pursue her own interests. Mac raised all sorts of objections when she suggested that he might prefer to spend his money on furnishing the house rather than buying more land in Scotland. He questioned the quality of the soil at Colney Park, and a frank exchange of views ensued. She insisted that only a blank refusal from him would dissuade her from going ahead. When this was not forthcoming, she submitted an offer of £9,550. This was accepted in May 1919 and Roderic and Iain's trustees stumped up the money.

The MacRobert property empire was growing fast. Douneside and Ranna were in trust for Alasdair, and Colney Park was in trust for Roderic and Iain. Mac still had his holdings in India, but it was his Scottish estate that kept him awake at night.

'Make things pleasant with your neighbour by making him pleased with himself. That is your duty as a social being,' he had written in his little book of everyday notes in April 1878. Yet less than forty years on, he found this pious ambition hard to live up to, when in 1911, he fell out with his neighbour Edward Reid. The ensuing legal case over whether or not the road between Douneside and West Town where Edward Reid farmed was a right of way dragged on for five years.

We can only hazard a guess as to why Mac put up a notice in 1910 at the point where the public road and the Douneside road met, stating that it was a private road to Douneside only. By this time, he would have been aware of Rachel's views on privacy and landownership and he may have been taking them into account. When Mr Reid continued to use the footpath, Mac wrote repeatedly to accuse him of trespass, and in June 1911, he warned him that proceedings would be raised if he persisted.

Reid sought the support of the Parish Council. He insisted that the road was a right of way, not a right of servitude. The Deeside District Committee of the County Council of Aberdeen was then dragged into the dispute since it was its duty to maintain the existence of a right of way. Reid then left them to the fight.

The court agreed, with some reservations, that there had been a right of way between Cushnie and Tarland in the 1800s. At the end of the century there was no objection to the new owner of West Town ploughing up the right of way, since there was no longer any need for wheeled traffic to use it. Since that time, the route between the two properties had been regularly used as a footpath and while Mac had not given him express permission to do so, John McRobert had even made two steps in the dyke for the greater convenience of the public.

Mac lost the case amid allegations that some witnesses had given false evidence. He immediately decided to seek advice as to whether an appeal against the decision might be successful. His advisor's opinion was that the judgement was legally flawed and that there were some fundamental errors in the Sheriff's judgement.

So Mac went back to court again, and in 1914, came the verdict he did not want to hear: his appeal had failed. The three judges seemed at times to be at variance with each other and admitted that there were facets of the case that made it exceptional. Yet despite making many criticisms of the judge, the witnesses and the Deeside District Committee, they refused to allow the appeal.

But Mac was defiant. He wrote in his notebook:

There are two ways of attaining an important end – force and perseverance.

And persevere he did. He appealed to the House of Lords but before the case could be heard, the dispute was finally settled out of court by a Minute of Agreement between Mac, the Reids and the Deeside District Committee. Mac agreed to provide an alternative footpath for walkers and the Deeside District Committee undertook to maintain part of it.

However, this was not quite the end of the saga. In February 1916, Mac wrote to the *Free Press* in Aberdeen, giving his side of the story. He said it was based on the facts, and that he wished to relay these to the wider public 'stripped of all the surplages' that had been reported. He claimed vehemently that he had been the victim of an injustice and that the Act of Parliament designed to facilitate the rights of the public had been used instead as an engine of oppression.

The case proved expensive for everyone involved. Lord Strathclyde, one of the three judges who heard the appeal, refused to grant the Deeside District Committee its extra-judicial expenses which totalled almost £700. On top of that, there were other clerical expenses to be met. Mac's legal bills cost him £3,066. 7s – plus a further £16. 7s to raise the appeal to the House of Lords.

Mac berated the Deeside District Committee for 'having the satisfaction of knowing that they have robbed me as effectively as if they had picked my pocket, without running any personal risk; wasted many months of valuable time and spent nearly £1,000 of ratepayers money in the pursuit of what one of their own chief witnesses has described as a 'concocted case'. The ratepayers do not seem to have realised that this concocted case was responsible for the addition of 2d to the rate'.

Mac bore such a grudge against the Deeside District Committee that he almost renounced his connections with Tarland. He accused it of committing a 'spoliation', a term in Scottish law for the intentional or negligent withholding, hiding, altering or destroying of evidence:

'The loss of so much valuable time, which cannot be made good, certainly has caused me keen regret,' he wrote, 'but that also is insignificant compared to the distress induced by the spectacle of a public body, at the bidding of an intriguing clique, forcing themselves into a private dispute and invoking the aid of the law, by not over scrupulous methods, to perpetrate what can only be described as a spoliation.'

Such were the intricacies of the case and the issues involved, that the battle fought in court is still being cited as a landmark case in Right of Way legal proceedings.

All this took place at a time when Mac's focus was on supporting the war effort from India. While the Deeside District Committee may have found against him, the Government's diplomatic services viewed him in a more positive light. In 1917 Russia was in turmoil and there were signs that Germany's influence there was growing. Mac was encouraged to visit the Amir of Afghanistan whose country was strategically placed as a buffer between Russia and India. Though it was born of a promise made some years before, Mac's talks with the Afghan leader now took on an extra and more urgent significance.

CHAPTER 11

The Amir and Afghanistan

A truly remarkable man of great ability who displays a facility in arriving at decisions which is akin to genius.

At the beginning of the 20th century, as Mac noted in his diary, social reform was badly needed in Afghanistan. This was a country where the most common form of execution was to be fired from a cannon and where a culture of bribery and corruption got in the way of doing business. He also lamented the way that women were excluded from many aspects of life.

But Amir Habibullah Khan who succeeded to the throne of Afghanistan in 1901, embarked on a programme of change that encompassed a multitude of issues: religious, democratic, military, social and educational. He also wanted to develop international trade and make the working practices of his country's industries more efficient. His goal was to establish a centralised and absolute government in Afghanistan.

During an official visit to India in 1907, the Amir had asked Lord Minto, the Viceroy at that time, to introduce him to Mac who agreed to show the Afghan ruler his Cawnpore mills. What the Amir saw there convinced him that he should try to emulate Mac's success by modernising manufacturing.

The two men struck up a rapport and the Amir asked Mac's advice on how best to develop the industries of his country, in particular the woollen mills. Mac held him in high esteem as his words at the head of this chapter bear witness. He deputed James Miller, a construction engineer, to go to Kabul and 'undertake and supervise the erection and initial working of a modern woollen mill there and to act as technical advisor on any other engineering or building project for the Amir'.

Miller proved to be an excellent choice. In the years between the Amir's visit to Cawnpore and Mac's to Afghanistan, he supervised the laying of a pipeline to bring water to Kabul City. He is credited with building the first

Clock Tower there in 1911. This was a great step forward, since the Afghans had to rely on the position of the sun and the firing of a gun to know what time it was. Miller was also responsible for setting up an irrigation system for the gardens of the Amir's many palaces: more importantly, this brought about dramatic improvements in the country's agriculture.

Mac himself turned down two invitations from the Amir to visit Afghanistan before agreeing to go, at the urging of the British government, in 1918. It was at a time when, according to the Calcutta newspaper, *The Statesman*, Germany was trying to bring Afghanistan into the war. The notes in Mac's diary show that he agreed with this assessment of the situation and he expressed his disquiet at the presence of Germans in the country. Yet despite the friendly overtures from Berlin, Amir Habibullah succeeded in keeping Afghanistan out of the conflict.

When he set off on what was described as a 'private visit', Mac was suffering from malaria, probably picked up on his long trip to Bangalore, Calcutta and Bombay shortly before. Ironically, this seems to have been a vacation on the instructions of his doctors who deemed he was suffering from overwork. He was accompanied by Logie Watson, his fellow Aberdonian and a partner in Cooper Allan and Co, who had been appointed a Member of the Council of the Lieutenant Governor for making Laws and Regulations.

If proof were ever needed that the world is a small place, at one of their first stops en route the travellers bumped into the son of 'Banker Thomson', whom Mac, still sulking, claimed had been an untruthful witness in the right of way case back home in Aberdeenshire.

In his diary, Mac describes the difficulties of obtaining a permit for travel through the Khyber Pass. He paints a colourful picture of the fort of Landi Kotal, the HQ of the Khyber Rifles, whose commander, Captain McCracken, hailed from Prestwick in the west of Scotland. The place, he wrote, teemed with humanity: the strategically located fortress was home to legions of tradesmen who earned their living servicing its needs. It was also 'absolutely packed with donkeys, camels, hens, puppies etc.'. With his usual keen eye for detail, he notes how 'the inhabitants vigilantly watch for sunset, wash their hands and pray to Mecca.'

The *Calcutta Statesman* recognised the significance of the visit:

During the past few years, Englishmen and Americans have been entering the employment of the Amir in increasing numbers with a view to running the electrical power plant and other enterprises which this up-to-date ruler has started, but all told, the white population of Kabul has never probably at any time exceeded a dozen. Very occasionally a diplomatic mission is dispatched by the Government of India, but for two Cawnpore merchants to pay an informal visit to Kabul as guests of His Majesty is quite unprecedented. The visit, from which these gentlemen have just returned, has also been paid in time of war. It has been explained with the utmost elaborateness both by them and by others, that their visit was for a purely business object, and had no diplomatic significance, but while this view may be accepted universally, it is almost certain that its results are highly unlikely to be confined to business achievement. The episode in the business development of Afghanistan may easily prove also a landmark in the political relations between that country and India.

Mac's diary of the trip provides a vivid snapshot of the political, social and economic situation in Afghanistan at the time. The country covered 220,000 square miles and was home to 5,000,000 people. Lying between Russia and India, Afghanistan's geographical position was seen by many countries as strategically important. Britain in particular, regarded it as an essential buffer between those two countries, and with the importance of India to its empire in mind, London was determined to find a way to exercise some control over it. At the end of the 2nd Afghan war in 1880, Britain had agreed to give the country financial aid and help in warding off foreign aggression, winning in return, the right to direct Afghanistan's relationships with other countries. The main threats were thought to come from the Germans, who in the years leading up to World War I, were perceived in diplomatic circles to be dangerously active in the Middle East. They had constructed the new Baghdad railway which made Iraq and Iran accessible for trade, and the Russians too had built a line right up to their frontier with Afghanistan.

At a time when the whole world was in turmoil, Mac's thoughts often strayed home to Europe. On 30 March 1918, in one of the first entries he made in his diary after his arrival in Afghanistan, he noted gloomily that the news from St Quentin, which was in the front line in France, was dire. Victory was now drawing closer, but in a disastrous week for Britain all advances had been lost along with 600 guns, 100 tanks, and countless lives. The offensive Mac referred to ultimately saw the Germans defeated and heralded the beginning of the end of the First World War.

Mac though had to apply himself to the task in hand and quickly recognised that, in trying to improve the economy of the country, there were many obstacles to overcome.

The infertile land and the lack of farming systems meant there were few, if any, prosperous farmers.

Although Mac was not there to help improve agriculture, his knowledge of land management derived from his early visits to his family in New Brunswick and then from his experiences at Douneside, meant that he was able to converse knowledgeably with the Amir on the subject and proffer his advice. For example, he suggested that 'applications of basic slag may be beneficial' to increase the fertility of the land. This, he said, had certainly improved the quality of the fields at Douneside.

Mac's diary contains many other observations of farming practices in Afghanistan. He and Logie Watson were fascinated to see how trenches were prepared for growing melons and cucumbers and a building where raisins were being dried caught their eye. He also noted:

Alfalfa grass is cut green for fodder.

The land around Kabul grows oats, wheat, barley, apples, pears, cherries, peaches, plums – and there are vineyards.

The Amir seems to have a passion for building palaces and the luxuriant gardens where 'verbena, phlox and fruit trees grow, are made possible by the irrigation systems being set up.

The country is thriving' wrote Mac in his diary. He also noted that electricity was being installed in the old palace.

The Government charges for water from the new canals.

Mac was interested in how the land was managed and recognised the short-comings of Afghan farming methods. 'The landlord,' he wrote, 'holds his land in perpetuity and leases it to tenants (who have no security of tenure and may be turned off at any time) to be cultivated. The proprietor pays the land tax, provides the seed and receives three quarters of the produce. The tenants provide the labour and generally speaking, two men and a bullock can cultivate twenty acres. The reward is one quarter of the produce.'

The Amir had failed in an experiment to improve the quality of wool used in the mills: the eight Merino rams and 200 ewes he imported all died. The cattle were in poor condition too, Mac observed.

He recognised that one of the barriers to future industrialisation was the lack of fuel to generate power. Despite offers of a reward for anyone who found one, no coal seams were found in the country.

The prime purpose of Mac's visit was to advise the Amir on the development of Afghanistan's textile industries. Although the mills there turned out cloth for all purposes, their main function was to provide clothing for the Army, just as the Cawnpore Mill had done so successfully in India. Mac and Watson were also commissioned to tour factories producing other goods before reporting their findings to the Amir.

The seven young Afghans who met them on their arrival in Afghanistan, complete with seven-seater motor car and five-ton Albion lorry, were accompanied by an interpreter named Khaligdad Khan. Back in 1885, at the conference at Rawalpindi between the Amir and Lord Dufferin, Mac had described the Afghans as 'ferocious looking fellows', and as his diary shows, he was still of the same opinion.

The two Scots found themselves escorted at all times by these Afghans and were allowed little freedom of movement during their visit. Mac found that Russians, on the other hand, were allowed to roam freely and even take photographs. Many were employed as tile makers, painters and masons. He worried too that if the German army invaded Russia, it would quickly push on into Afghanistan just as it had done in Turkey which would have unpredictable consequences for India. He and Watson exchanged views on the Germans with the Crown Prince, although the latter's views were discreetly not recorded.

When they arrived in Jalalabad, they were told that the Amir was incapacitated and that they would have to wait two or three days to see him. Nevertheless, he sent them food and his 'solicitous enquiries'. Both Mac and Watson were also dogged by ill health and almost died when noxious fumes from a brazier filled the place in which they were staying. So ill were they that Mac pondered making a codicil to his will.

When at last His Majesty was well enough to receive them, he was pleased to accept their gifts of tea, a silver salver and cigarettes. Unfortunately His Majesty thought that Mac's cherished photos of Rachel and home were also a gift, and in a letter home to Rachel, Mac lamented their loss. During this meeting the Amir showed that he was extremely knowledgeable about the manufacturing industries and how they had developed since his visit to Cawnpore in 1907. He also praised James Miller and was concerned that he had not returned from leave: Mac's chosen emissary was suffering from ill health and both he and his wife were also grieving the death of their son. In later years, Mac hired Miller again to undertake turbine work at the New Egerton Mill at Dhariwal. When he retired to Scotland, he and his wife went to live in Forres in Moray and became frequent visitors to Douneside.

Mac's notes from his tour of the factories and mills paint a vivid picture of the manufacturing industries in Afghanistan at the time:

Tailors use Singer Sewing Machines.

The power looms are neglected and out of order but hand looms a great success.

Khaki dye is made with Pomegranate, Walnut and a powdered nut called Mazoo, probably the cone of Juniper or Cypress. It is said to come from Persia.

The cloths produced are most creditable.

There are workshops for ... accoutrements and equipment including a rifle and shell factory, an ammunition factory and a foundry. ... a printing press, litho printing and bookbinding facility. They make leather buttons; have an electro plating department, make full dress helmets, scabbards and elaborate railings for a Palace.

On a visit to the Tannery on 17 April 1918, he notes that 'the leather is tanned with a mixture of almond bark and pomegranates giving a very good colour'.

These tanners made not only boots for the army, but also harnesses and saddles for horses. They supplied boots and shoes to His Majesty's harem: an industry in itself because the Amir had 200 wives and 100 children.

In their report Mac and Watson suggested how industrial output could be increased by 50 per cent: a worsted plant could be built at Peshawar and a spindle cotton mill could be set up for the manufacture of hosiery. By way of thanks for how well they had been treated during their trip, Mac generously offered to train a group of men in Cawnpore at his own expense.

At what they assumed was their final interview, on Mac's birthday, they too were rewarded. Mac received two gold bracelets and a locket containing photos of His Majesty for Rachel. He himself received a speaking tube from the Amir, a device through which speech could be transmitted over a long distance. And there were yet more gifts for the two Scots: a magnificent gold watch and a massive silver drinking cup complete with cover and tray for Mac; a fine enamelled cigarette case and cigar holder for Logie Watson. Each man also received four suit-lengths of tweed, a bale of carpets, and a horse with a promise that it would be delivered to them in Cawnpore. Mac was touched that the Amir placed his hand on his head and gave him his blessing.

The next day, they were suddenly recalled to the palace: the Amir had other things he wished to say. He presented them with five signed photos and asked Mac to send him his own photo of Douneside in exchange. He even laid down what he wanted written on the back.

The unexpected surprise was his award to Mac of a gold medal, the Honour of Afghanistan. As he wrote later in letters to friends and relations, he was happy that he had accomplished what he set out to do during their six week stay. He had been overwhelmed by His Majesty's kindness and the decoration he had been given. As he wrote in his diary, he remained realistic about the state of the Afghan nation:

On the whole, I am going away with a very different opinion of the country and the people from the one I carried up with me. Money seems plentiful, and expensive clothes, boots and furniture are in evidence everywhere. The blot is the seclusion of women: and the craze of the Amir for building palaces. In the long run, the latter is bound to cause discontent. There is no doubt that the truth is handled with economy, even parsimony, and that corruption is almost universal. The latter is a veritable canker. The object does not seem to be to buy in the best market, but to buy so that the commission of the buying agent shall be as high as possible. This makes honest business next to impossible. The honest trader is not in favour. I am also apprehensive about the large number of Austrian and German – ostensibly escaped – prisoners that are trickling through from Russia, they will in the end, prove a grave political danger.

The men arrived back in Cawnpore in June 1918 to the pleasing news that Watson had been awarded a knighthood. Later, in August of that year, Rachel wrote to thank the Amir for 'his gifts and the gracious hospitality he had afforded Sir Alec'. She added that 'the children will be proud to speak of the honour and would wish to convey their thanks through herself, their mother.'

Rachel was at home in Tarland, and there later that year, she received a telegram from Andrew Farquharson of Finzean to tell her that the Great War was over. The Union Jack was promptly raised in celebration on the tower at Douneside and the children were taken for a drive down to Tarland as the church bells pealed out to welcome peace. Flags were flying everywhere and a bonfire was lit near the church to celebrate the occasion.

Sadly there was no happy ending to the story of Mac's friendship with the Amir. In the small hours of the morning on the 20 February 1919 Habibullah Khan was shot in the ear while he slept in his royal tent. Mac received the news from one of his men who was working at the Khalat-Ul-Seraj palace and who had been in conversation with the Amir just a few days before his departure. The monarch's body was taken back to Jalalabad where it was buried that afternoon. Although the Amir's brother, Nasrullah, was suspected of being involved in the assassination plot, he took the throne before being ousted only a week later by Habibullah's third son, Amanullah.

One of Amanullah's first acts was to order the Cawnpore engineers home to India on twelve months' unpaid leave. All engineering works would be suspended until he had settled affairs of state.

CHAPTER 12

Bringing It All Together

To thine own self be true, and it must follow, as the night the day, thou canst not then be false to any man.

Polonius's advice to his son Laertes in *Hamlet* was one of many quotes that Mac copied into his notebooks. Presumably he saw it as a sentiment by which to live: certainly throughout his career he was jealous of his good reputation.

None of Cawnpore's merchant princes escaped criticism as they seized opportunities to build up their businesses and make their fortunes, but Mac found any aspersions cast upon his integrity hard to cope with. An incident that aroused his fury concerned one of the Empire's most feted war heroes, Frederick Roberts. Roberts came from Cawnpore: in fact he had been born in 1832 in a bungalow inside the compound at the Cawnpore Woollen Mills, close by the Tamarind tree.

His father, Sir Abraham, had risen to become the Commander of the East India Company's Bengal European Regiment, but Frederick's own military career was even more glorious. During the Indian Mutiny, in January 1858, he won the Victoria Cross at Khudaganj for his bravery in saving the life of one of his locally-recruited sepoy soldiers and capturing a standard from the rebels during fierce hand-to-hand fighting. Later, as supreme commander in South Africa, he played a decisive role in bringing the 2nd Boer War to an end. And it was in the aftermath of this military triumph that Mac found himself in trouble.

In his capacity as President of the Upper India Chamber of Commerce, Mac had sent a message to 'Bobs', as Rudyard Kipling called him. It read simply: 'Your birthplace salutes you.' Delighted at receiving these congratulations, especially as they were the first to reach him after the hostilities ended, 'Bobs' telegraphed back: 'Many thanks for your welcome message'.

But Mac had failed to consult the members of the Upper India Chamber before sending the message. They first learned that their President had sent congratulations on their behalf, when Mac used the pages of the *Pioneer* newspaper to inform a wider audience. Only then, on 3 March 1900, did he write to the Chamber's secretary:

Dear Sir,

On 28th ultimo on arrival of the news of Cronje's surrender I took the liberty of wiring to Field Marshal Lord Roberts at Paarldelberg: 'Your birthplace salutes you'.

I did this as President of the Chamber of Commerce representing the Commercial Community. The following reply has just been received from Lord Roberts:

Many thanks for your welcome message.

I shall be obliged if you will kindly circulate this among the Members of the Committee for information.

Sammy Johnson, Managing Director at the Muir Mill, is said to have been the man who more than any other brought out the worst in Mac. He was annoyed that Mac had not observed the rules and consulted members first and seized this opportunity to attack him. Johnson was particularly angry that Mac had made use of his position as President without the knowledge and approval of the committee. Others saw Mac's message in a positive light. One member wrote that Cawnpore should be 'proud to be the birth-place of a general who has so materially changed the outlook of the war for the better. ... Mr Johnson's note of dissent certainly does not sound well'. For a time a barrage of letters filled the correspondence columns of the *Pioneer* newspaper, but the Cawnpore community stood behind Mac and the incident eventually blew over.

Another attack on his integrity was of a more serious nature. It did not help that it cropped up after Mac had gone through difficult times at the New Egerton mills at Dhariwal. In 1910, fire – always a threat in a woollen mill – broke out there. Raw materials and finished goods were destroyed, although the manufacturing plant escaped the worst of the damage and work could still be carried out. Then, when the rebuilding programme was almost complete, a whirlwind brought down the three-storey extension. This setback and other delays meant that it was only just up and running when the First World War was declared, but then the mills there and in Cawnpore rose to the occasion. Despite a shortage of labour, Dhariwal, which only fulfilled government orders, worked flat out.

So it was particularly galling for Mac, when in 1917, he was asked by the Department of Commerce and Industry to prove that he was not making excess profits on his government contracts. Mac replied that the increase in production he had ordered to satisfy the army's demands for clothing had taken its toll on both his machinery and his labour force, but since he had made savings from mass production, he would refund some £23,000 to the government. Once again Mac felt that his integrity was being impugned, and he was especially incensed by accusations that the refund was merely a sop to a profiteer's conscience.

In his defence, he pointed out that by devoting the output of Dhariwal to the army contract the company had had to forsake its regular customers, and that as a patriotic gesture the rates he was charging were the same as in pre-war years. No one was surprised when Mac's own newspaper, the Indian *Daily Telegraph*, took up the cudgels on his behalf:

If India is to support the war effort in this way, it is reasonable to expect the large industrial organisations to anticipate an Excess Profits Tax by voluntary contributions.

They would be following the example of the Directors of the Cawnpore Woollen Mill who have already made a substantial contribution to government funds.

To subscribe to the State's loans in wartime is certainly patriotic, but a voluntary refund of profits is more, it is philanthropic, and the C.W.M. has done magnificently in thus giving up the equivalent of £23,000.

In a further gesture of patriotic support, the company invested £100,000 in Exchequer Bonds and the British War Loan and an additional £100,000 in the Indian War Loan.

Mac eventually did find the gratitude that he felt was due to him. At a dinner held in November 1918 by the Cawnpore Chamber of Commerce to mark the Armistice, the guest speaker, the Lieutenant Governor of the United Provinces of Agra and Oudh, Sir Harcourt Butler, paid tribute to Cawnpore's contribution to the war effort:

> Your great mills and concerns which employ over 30,000 hands have been working night and day to provide munitions and supplies for our brave armies.

He added:

> I must mention specifically that the Cawnpore Woollen Mill and the New Egerton Mills under the patriotic guidance of Sir Alexander MacRobert whose name will ever stand foremost in the history of Cawnpore have, since the beginning of the War, invested no less than £1,175,000 in the various forms of war loan.

Sir Harcourt went on to praise the pioneering work by Mac and Cawnpore's other industrialists in setting up *Ganjs* for their workers. These and the other benefits enjoyed by their Indian employees had ensured their loyalty throughout the war years, enabling the mills to fulfil their orders.

In his reply at that same dinner, Mac paid tribute to the Armed Forces whose bravery and sacrifice had secured peace and he acknowledged the debt owed to them by the nation. He felt that he too, had taken some brave decisions, showing his support for the war effort by dedicating the production of the New Egerton Mill to supplying the war effort with its requirements.

In recognition of his services, and also perhaps as a reward for his diplomatic foray into Afghanistan, Mac was awarded the KBE in the New Year's honours list in 1919.

After the war, mill owners were faced with a new set of challenges. Production had gone back to pre-war levels and much of their machinery and plant had suffered from constant use. They felt that an Excess Profit Tax, which the government was still considering introducing, would be an unfair imposition after all they had done for the war effort. Even so Mac continued to support his adopted country by subscribing to a second Indian War loan.

Although political activity in the area was escalating and bad feeling was growing towards the colonial industrialists, Mac chose this moment to take a radical step: in 1920 he decided to bring his six businesses into one conglomerate to be named the British India Corporation.

Since his rescue of the woollen mill during his early years in Cawnpore, Mac had kept an eye to the future and to every new business opportunity. He had bought up the New Egerton Woollen Mill at Dhariwal not only to eliminate a competitor but also so that he could greatly increase production at a time when demand almost exceeded supply. His next step was to install a thermal plant steam engine at New Egerton to help the business grow even further. Another prudent move was the purchase of the woollen business side of the rival Elgin Mills, along with its machinery.

He also began to diversify into other industries that were already established in the area. Before Mac's arrival in India, political changes and the abolition of the East India Company had opened up new opportunities, as had improvements to the country's infrastructure, especially the railway system. The American Civil War which broke out in 1861, brought about the expansion of the cotton industry in India. Transatlantic links with Manchester were severed during the conflict, and the mills there which had been dependent on America for their supplies of raw material, turned to India to fulfil their needs. But Indian cotton was of inferior quality and Manchester now demanded better. The Indian Government took up the challenge and offered incentives to improve cotton cultivation and boost economic prosperity in the north of the country.

It was the station master of the East India Railway in Cawnpore, Frederick Buist, who realised what an opportunity was being missed. He saw mountains of baled cotton stacked high in the sidings waiting to be exported by train, yet he realised no one was spinning it into cloth in the city. He approached businessmen in the area, both Indian and British, with the idea of forming a Cawnpore Cotton Committee.

As a result, in December 1864, the Elgin Cotton Spinning and Weaving Company was registered. It was named, as was the custom of the day, after the Viceroy, Lord Elgin. Thus, Cawnpore became the site of the first up-country cotton mill in India: but the problems that arose in putting the business on its feet proved insurmountable, and after a few years of struggle a petition was raised in 1870 for it to be wound up.

Two of the Elgin Mills' founder members, Hugh Maxwell and Gavin Jones, however, believed that the enterprise still had potential. Maxwell was the only bidder when the mill was sold at auction and he bought it for a song, at roughly one third of its value. Gavin Jones was appointed manager and within a year he had turned the Elgin Mill into a profitable business. Long after Mac's time, after passing through several hands, it was acquired by the BIC.

Maxwell and Jones quarrelled and parted company in 1872, but two years later, with some friends and acquaintances, Jones took the first step towards opening up Cawnpore to industrialisation on a grand scale. His idea was to build a rival cotton spinning and weaving mill. He was the only member of the consortium with any knowledge of textiles and just happened to own a suitable piece of land for the site of the proposed enterprise. The Muir Mill was duly launched and became renowned for the superior quality of its cloth. This was the company that had hired Mac as a chemist in 1884 but then found it no longer needed his services when he arrived to take up the post. By 1897, he was its largest shareholder.

The first cotton factory acquired by the BIC was the Cawnpore Cotton Mills Co. Ltd. John Harwood its founder, came to Cawnpore in 1880 to work at the Elgin Mills, but he soon seized the opportunity to set up a rival company. Its trade name was 'Kakomi', which Harwood boasted stood for 'unsurpassed' quality.

The grandly-named Empire Engineering Co Ltd was another of the first six companies that the BIC took under its umbrella. Founded in the 1890s by Gavin Jones and his son Tracy who had trained as a mining engineer in Rhodesia, the business was slow to take off but it eventually became the largest and most progressive engineering shop in Upper India. The secret of its success lay in its ability to manufacture anything from bolts to railway bridges in its many foundries and sawmills. The firm capitalised on the continued expansion of the railway system, and, in accordance with the philosophy of the nationalist Swadeshi movement and its campaign to make India self-supporting, it ploughed back the profits into buying up-to-date machinery.

Perhaps the most interesting of all the businesses that became part of the BIC – the conglomerate was not officially incorporated until 1922 – was Cooper Allen and Co. Ltd. Mac had known William Cooper and George Allen since he arrived in India. They had set up as managing agents a few years earlier. In doing so, they were following a tradition established in the 18th century. While the British East India Company was responsible for exports such as indigo, cotton, tea, saltpetre, leather, spices and opium, managing agents worked on commission, importing goods such as machinery, into the country. Gradually they became involved in the management of estates and plantations and soon moved into fledgling industries like the railways.

Cooper Allen was no exception, and the Cawnpore Woollen Mills was one of the many businesses they managed. They had appointed Mac as their representative there when the job that had originally brought him to India failed to materialise.

Managing agents often invested their own capital in the companies for which they acted and they could also conduct two-way trade. The invention of the electric telegraph and improvements in other forms of international communications enabled them to keep abreast of changing market prices and consequently to expand into providing services such as insurance and banking and opening employment agencies. There was nothing complicated or even sophisticated about the way they ran their businesses: the managing agents prided themselves on being 'hands-on' and made all the important decisions themselves.

Meanwhile Gavin Jones had yet another idea. In 1879, he noticed that the government Harness and Saddlery factory in Allahabad was booming. It was run by Colonel John Stewart of the Bengal Artillery, the scion of a landowning family from Perthshire in Scotland. The Military Seminary at Addiscombe near Croydon in Surrey where he trained was regarded as the Sandhurst of the Indian Army, whilst family connections were still vital for those who wanted to join the ranks of the elite. Stewart was fortunate that a member of his family was chairman of the East India Company and this helped him to secure a coveted posting to the Bengal Artillery in 1852. However, he was not required to use his fighting skills when the Indian

Mutiny broke out. Instead he was sent to Allahabad as a logistics man, where his responsibilities were to feed, clothe and provide ammunition for the troops and their animals, and to ensure that the army and its equipment always arrived where they were needed. Here, too, he was able to exploit the old boy network.

Frederick Roberts, the hero Mac had controversially written to at the end of the Boer War, had trained at Addiscombe with Stewart. He stayed with him at Allahabad while he was organising the Viceroy's Grand Tour which followed the transfer of power from the East India Company to the British government. Roberts gave Stewart the job of supplying 150 large and elaborate tents, 500 camels, 500 bullocks, 100 bullock carts, 40 riding elephants and 527 coolies whose task was to carry the glass windows of the tents. Stewart did this so efficiently that his superiors sent him to Cawnpore to organise the Artillery there and this is where he saw his opportunity.

The needs of an Army conducting warfare in Indian terrain were many and varied. They included tents, ropes, harness, saddlery, boots and shoes. When Stewart found that he was heavily dependent on Europe for supplies of raw materials, he decided to examine the feasibility of sourcing and manufacturing them locally. The proposal led to his being given permission by the government to develop a state-owned tannery.

One of the main problems he faced was to find suitable hides, since those that were available in Cawnpore were inferior to those imported from abroad. Another was to find ways to bring the tanning industry up-to-date. Traditionally the Cawnpore settlement had been supplied with leather goods by the leather workers who were known as *Chamars*, but their production methods were primitive. They hung skins in the corner of their huts and treated them with tannin made from the bark of the Babul tree which grew wild in the area. The leather produced in this way fell short of the standards expected by the military, so Stewart spent two years in Britain researching the new techniques that would enable Cawnpore's tanneries to compete.

He returned to Cawnpore in 1869 full of enthusiasm and turned the small arsenal depot there into the Government Harness and Saddlery Factory. It was soon supplying all the leather equipment for the British armies in the East. By 1873 the factory employed more than 2,000 workers and the leather they produced was good enough to win a bronze medal at the Leipzig Exhibition. As a result, Cawnpore became a hub of the leather industry and Mac invested in another business set up at the same time as Stewart's factory, the North West Tannery Company. Gavin Jones had noticed this business was going through bad times and was strapped for cash. However, his ambitious plans for it were thwarted by Mac whose injection of cash allowed it to continue trading. It became the largest and most up-to-date tannery in the East and was also incorporated into the BIC.

The boom in leather production gave Gavin Jones the idea of setting up a business to manufacture boots for the army. He put his proposal to Cooper and Allen who had the ear of the Viceroy and other high ranking army officials. They took it on and were duly awarded a contract in 1881. John Stewart was appointed to supervise the factory to protect the government's interests, and in later years it was said to be 'the largest army boot and equipment factory in the world'.

When Cooper Allen became part of the BIC, Mac was disappointed to discover that the boot factory was not contributing to the business, thanks to a clause in the contract with the government designed to prevent the owners making unduly high profits. Since government sales made up 61 per cent of the company's turnover and prices were fixed, the enterprise was struggling. Cooper suggested that the way to return his company to profitability would be to diversify further into the cotton, woollen and sugar industries: this would dilute the dependence on government sales.

The formal amalgamation took place on 1 January 1922 and the firms began to trade under the name of the British India Corporation. Mac believed that the activities of each company would complement each other and that economies of scale would give the new conglomerate an advantage over its competitors. The company's policy was to be 'Made in India by Indians for India'.

Mac was not to get the chance to remain at the helm of his new enterprise for much longer. He had endured great stresses and strains in setting it up and had done so alone without a wife by his side because Rachel had decided to stay in Scotland to bring up their three sons. He was sixty-seven, his health was failing and more troubles lay ahead.

CHAPTER 13

Death of A Merchant Prince

He will long be missed in the United Provinces as a great leader of good causes, a generous benefactor – a staunch and lionhearted friend.

The beginning of 1922, when the British India Corporation came into being, was a time of mixed fortunes for Mac.

In January, the news broke that he had been awarded a baronetcy. Rachel claimed he had not told her that he was to receive this recognition in the India List of the King's New Year's Honours, but Mac always maintained that she had known in advance, saying she had opened the Prime Minister's letter about the award although it had been addressed to him. He, on the other hand, had only learned of it on New Year's Day itself in a telegram from the Viceroy. In a letter to Rachel he fussed about the details:

I am now concerned to know if the recommendation came from India or originated at home.

He added:

I am looking forward to your report on the reception of the event which is naturally epoch making in the McRobert family. (By the way, I have thought of adopting the form MacRobert.)

He gave no reason for this decision, but he announced that he wished to be known as Sir Alexander MacRobert of Cawnpore and Cromar of the County of Aberdeen. Rachel wanted the Workman coat of arms to be incorporated into the new MacRobert one, but an official of the College of Arms in London advised against the idea:

It would not be advisable to introduce any position of the Workman coat into the MacRobert arms as you will of course be entitled to impale the Workman coat.

Mac adopted the Robertson coat of arms and Rachel was mollified by the news that the title was hereditary. Her father wrote that 'she had done pretty well for herself as far as wealth, position and titles were concerned in marrying McRobert.'

Business associates in India showered Mac with congratulations. One, signing himself only 'a Merchant Banker', wrote to the press:

> The Baronetcy has been awarded in recognition of your meritorious services to Government as well as the public. It is a matter of great pride to the people of the United Provinces and especially the share holders of the BIC to see their esteemed citizen and chairman honoured with such a high honour.

The Directors and staff of the BIC were quick to welcome and recognise the 'signal honour conferred on him by His Majesty': 'Only those who have had the privilege of working with you can adequately appreciate how well deserved this rare distinction is. …'

But the good news of the baronetcy was offset by the bad news from India, where there was growing unrest in politics, and most crucially for Mac, in the labour market.

His problems began when a message addressed to the manager was posted outside the New Egerton Mill. The writers protested that although the firm had made substantial profits in 1921, no annual increments or bonuses had been paid to the Indian workers. Both hours and the number of employees had been cut and the result, the letter claimed, was that while the Europeans prospered, local people faced hardship. Now they had had enough: 'Being much tired of your injustice, we hereby express our thoughts of censure for your menial efforts.'

The letter contained something far more worrying than even these bitter accusations: a threat to burn down the mill. The BIC's directors responded by adding two Indian patrols to the nightly fire inspections by its European staff and the number of spot checks on the buildings was also increased.

Despite these new security measures, the alarm sounded at 9.00 am on 12 April. By 10.30 the blaze was fierce, the mill's roof had cracked and its walls were bulging. When the fire was eventually brought under control, investigators discovered that it had broken out in three or four different places at once and that it had been started deliberately. Despite European and Indian staff working 'splendidly' together, extensive damage had been caused to the machinery.

The manager believed that the attack was the result of anti-British feeling and civil unrest fomented by the Akali movement, a group of Sikhs campaigning for the right to run their own places of worship. In a letter to Mac, he expressed the hope that 'When something really serious happens, the Government will perhaps do something to crush the anti-European movement which is causing so much trouble throughout the country'.

These early stirrings of the campaign for independence must have come as a shock to Mac who had been ahead of his time in his concern for the welfare of the people who worked in his mills and factories. Only a dozen years before, the workers from the same mill had sent him a very different letter, couched in the most flowery and effusive terms, to congratulate him on his knighthood:

Honoured Sir,

We your humble servants, the Indian Members of Dhariwal Mill staff, beg leave to respectfully offer you our hearty congratulations on the signal honour that has been conferred upon you by our Gracious Sovereign the Emperor of India.

By the deep and unfailing interest you have always taken in our welfare, you have endeared yourself to every heart, and we feel very proud and happy to see that our Kind Master has been honoured by His Majesty with the grant of distinguished order of Knighthood.

We gratefully beg to acknowledge and recall it at this moment the fact that during your high office of Managing Directorship of the Mills you have always been good enough to do and have done everything that was required to ameliorate the condition of the Indian Staff.

It is through your benevolence and kindness that we are provided with a very necessary and important institution – the school – which you have given us for the use of our children. ...

We are provided with Pucca houses in place of the old mud quarters.

You have favoured us with the grant of the system of Bonus and you have very generously improved the position of the Indian staff both materially and financially.

We also beg to express our thankfulness for the great loan that you have conferred upon us by establishing a much needed institution Dhariwal Co-operative Credit Society Ltd.

These are Sir but few of the many favours which you have done to improve the lot of your Indian staff.

We are proud to be members of a service which has at the helm kind and sympathetic Masters like yourself and like our present kind manager Mr J.W. Armstrong to whose untiring energy, wisdom and whole-hearted devotion to work is due to present, prosperous and much advanced condition of the Mills.

We again beg to tender our respectful congratulations upon the distinguished mark of His Majesty's favour and sincerely pray for a long life and health to enjoy the honour.

We also beg to offer a poor and insignificant present in token of respect and remembrance of the High honour conferred upon you, hoping you will be good enough to accept it.

In this febrile atmosphere, it is not perhaps surprising that Mac's thoughts turned to home. In February 1922, he wrote to Thomas Jamieson at the laboratory of the Aberdeen City Analyst to say that he was hoping to develop the production of ramie, a substitute for flax. British firms like Richards & Co, the textile business that stood next to the house where he was born, were facing the imminent demise of the flax industry. Farmers in the United Kingdom were unwilling to grow the lint from which it is derived and Richards was no longer able to source the raw material from Russia, their sole supplier for the past six years.

Jamieson replied that he thought India could fill the breach, but added that he was worried by the stories he was hearing about sinister goings-on in India. 'Haste ye hame', he wrote.

Mac returned on leave that April, but he was now a sick man. His health had suffered from his relentless drive to achieve his ambitions. He had ignored advice from his doctor Sir Henry Gray to slow down after an operation to remove his gall bladder, some gallstones and his appendix at the Kepplestone Nursing Home in Aberdeen in October 1921. So ill was he that he was not expected to recover, but he amazed Rachel and his doctors with his return to health. Despite having undergone this major surgery, he had insisted on returning to India to preside at the AGM of his infant British India Corporation. Ill health continued to dog him and following a bout of flu he was diagnosed with angina and ordered to take six months rest. He set about putting his affairs in order in a bid to minimise inheritance tax.

On 22 June 1922 Mac had planned to attend the funeral of a friend in Aberdeen but his plans were thwarted when his car refused to start. Rachel was despatched to get the part fixed. She returned to find that he had had an attack of angina, which he confessed to her was the worst yet; but after a visit from the doctor, the pain eased off and he felt able to eat his dinner.

Later, as Rachel was dining downstairs with two of Mac's friends, she heard a faint ring of his bell. She rushed up to find him in the throes of a heart attack. The 'uncrowned King of Cawnpore' died in her arms.

Mac's death was not unexpected. Her father told his sister that Rachel had been telling him that Mac had been suffering regular bouts of pain.

In the days that followed his death, Rachel received 240 letters of condolence and many more followed. As a token of its regard and respect for their benefactor, Aberdeen University allowed Mac's remains to rest in the University Court room prior to his funeral service. His coffin was made of oak and was garlanded with flowers from all over the world. The Principal Sir George Adam Smith offered thanks for Mac's devotion to duty and his consideration for others. He praised his strength of mind and character and his 'enlightened liberality'. Crowds lined the route of the funeral procession from Marischal College to Allenvale Cemetery where the graveside service was conducted by Reverend Professor Cowan. Those who lowered their friend to his final resting place, beside Georgina and her mother, included his neighbour Lord Aberdeen, his lawyer J. Younger Collie and his friends from India, Sir William Cooper and CT Allen.

Across the seas, at Christ Church, Cawnpore, Canon Fisher conducted a memorial service in which he spoke of Mac as a man who despite his success, had never lost the common touch:

> He took the trouble to preserve the personal touch – he knew his people and therefore knew their needs … His best gift to Cawnpore is the example and memory of an exceptionally kind hearted Christian gentleman with a simple faith and a steady determination to duty which in all the thronging claims of business insisted on his personal attention to the needs and the welfare of his fellow man.

Mac's obituaries in the newspapers paid tribute to the man who had risen from such humble beginnings in a tenement in Aberdeen to travel to the courts of Amirs and to take a seat amongst the movers and shakers of the British Empire.

They all praised his business acumen, but the *Calcutta Statesman* also highlighted the intellectual curiosity that had spurred him on to such success:

> He was a student to whom the acquisition of knowledge was an abiding passion.

Others remembered his enlightened attitude to his workers:

'In these days of political turmoil one is apt to forget what the country owes to the undemonstrative work of the true lovers of India like Sir Alexander', wrote one.

'The Lalimli settlement is a fine example of what a capitalist who loves his worker can and ought to do. On Sundays he can be found spending time with the lowliest of workers whose family budget is as important as his balance sheet,' said another.

A friend offered a more intimate glimpse of his character:

> He had too strong a personality to be without detractors. But neither in public nor in private was he known to speak against any persons. His reticence doubtless was sometimes misunderstood.

Everyone agreed that it was for his altruism and his philanthropy that he would be most fondly and enduringly remembered. In a letter to the then President of the Upper India Chamber of Commerce, Sir Harcourt Butler spoke for many:

The Government have frequently had the advantage of Sir Alexander's advice and his generous donations to public objects have won the admiration and esteem of all … He will long be missed in the United Provinces as a great leader of good causes, a generous benefactor and a staunch and lionhearted friend.

The obituaries listed his achievements. They recalled how, as President of the Upper India Chamber of Commerce, he had travelled extensively to congresses throughout the world where his speeches, always well-informed, had given out a powerful message.

They recorded the offices Mac had held in many of India's most prestigious organisations. He was a Governor of Roorkee Engineering College founded in the 1840s to train civil engineers in Northern India, especially those employed in the construction of the Ganges canal. He also held a similar position at the Agricultural College of Cawnpore, which became the Government Agricultural College in 1906. They remembered that Mac had been President of the Indian branch of the St John's Ambulance Association and that he was a member of the Legislative Council of the United Provinces of Agra and Oudh. His rapport with the people of the area, together with his wide knowledge of industry, meant his advice was much sought-after.

The Government also valued Mac's experience and expertise and listened to what he had to say. On one occasion, in December 1916, he was invited to share his opinions at a meeting of Industrial Commissioners. He said that the working classes in India were not ready for compulsory general education and definitely not for technical education. The best approach, he believed, would be for businesses to help raise the standard of living by offering better wages in return for better work. Then a desire for education would automatically follow.

'We all unconsciously try to live up to our environment,' he explained. 'There is a need for intelligent workers – however they are not at the stage of being proud of having done anything well.'

Universities recognised his contributions to business, engineering and society. At Allahabad he was made a Fellow in the Faculty of Science, while in 1912 Aberdeen awarded him an Honorary Doctorate of Laws for his work in improving the living conditions of the Indians and for endowing the cancer research fellowship in memory of Georgina.

In both Scotland and India he was remembered with gratitude by ordinary people too. He saw it as a duty – one that he obviously enjoyed – to encourage men to better themselves. His sound business instincts and genuine concern for the Indians amongst whom he lived enabled him to give them useful and practical advice on how to manage their family budgets and improve their lives. He was a pioneer in the provision of model villages and other amenities for his mill workers, but he did not stop there. On many a Sunday afternoon he was to be found sitting on the steps of their humble homes encouraging them to help themselves and improve their lot.

He took up this theme when in September 1917 he accepted the rare accolade of being elected an honorary member of the Aberdeen Chamber of Commerce. Citing the part Indians were playing in the Great War, he advocated home rule for the subcontinent. This was a goal to be reached carefully and slowly, but he had no doubt that 'should India be given the opportunity to develop its educational system and its politics it could have a great future.'

He never forgot his roots and those less fortunate than himself. Indeed, he was not too grand to take part in a ceremony organised in 1919 by a body known as the Stoneywood Useful Knowledge Association that he had belonged to in his younger days. On a hilltop above the grey North Sea at the unveiling of a memorial, he paid tribute to the 40 club members killed in the Great War, and quoted in their memory those famous and resonant lines from the Book of Ecclesiastes in the Bible: 'Let us now praise famous men and the fathers who begat us.'

In February 1917, he gave generously to Mrs Abbot's appeal for the Scottish Women's Hospital for War Service and to the church in the parish where he spent his formative years. He donated £5,000 to a convalescent home near the Stoneywood Paper Mill where he had begun his working life and another gift went to set up funds for pensioners in the neighbourhood.

A plaque commemorating his gift of valuable shares in his Indian mills and other acts of generosity used to hang at Woolmanhill Hospital in Aberdeen. On it was inscribed a drawing of that red Lalimli tree which stood in the grounds of the Cawnpore Mill. In January 1916, the Board of Directors admitted Mac and Rachel as life members of the corporation of the Royal Infirmary and Lunatic Asylum of Aberdeen to thank them for the donations they had made towards the deficit of the Infirmary accounts for the year 1914. Mac's reply to their letter of thanks was modest. He was reminded, he said, that it 'was a greater pleasure to give than to receive' though ever the businessman, he usually hedged about his donations with stringent conditions to ensure that they would provide benefits into the future.

Sorting out the affairs of a man of property can be a complex business, and Mac's proved more difficult than most, especially since his estate included his interests outside Scotland. The red tape and the political and industrial turmoil in India led to frustration and disagreements among the executors, who included Mac's lawyers, his nephew Arthur Lilley, Logie Watson and Rachel.

At home, they were forced to fight a long battle with the tax inspector before successfully establishing that Mac had been domiciled in India. The prize was worth the struggle: if they had lost the argument, much of Mac's fortune would have gone in death duties.

More problems arose because Mac had redrafted his will less than a year before he died. He left a fifth of his estate to Rachel and the same share to each of his three sons. The final tranche included legacies of £500 to the executors, one month's pay to the workers at the Cawnpore and Dhariwal mills, with much of the rest going to charitable causes. The executors had no reason to believe that he would not have paid his usual meticulous attention to the wording of his will, but some of its provisions were ruled to be invalid. One concerned the endowment of the Georgina McRobert Hospital in Cawnpore and another was intended to enable the proposed Technical Institute in Cawnpore to set up scholarships or to fund the building or extension of a museum there.

Eventually matters were settled. After tax had been paid, Mac's estate in the United Kingdom was valued at £264,552 1s 3d, the equivalent of £6,000,000 today. Later, his shares in the BIC realised around £1,000,000.

Rachel now found herself rich but alone, with an estate to run and three small sons to bring up.

CHAPTER 14

A Band of Brothers

That to live a happy life, one must live a dangerous one.

(The subject proposed for a debate at the young Alasdair MacRobert's school in 1926.)

Mac was dead and Cawnpore was without the man Sir James Meston, the Lieutenant Governor of the United Provinces, had described as its 'King'. Yet the survival of the MacRobert name and baronetcy seemed assured. Mac had three sons and a young widow, Rachel, who thanks to her enquiring mind and determination to succeed, looked set to become a woman of power and influence. Her immediate challenge however, was to bring up her family single-handed. She had no other close relations at hand to help.

The early life of her first-born was chronicled in a series of 'diaries' entitled *The Journals of Alasdair Workman MacRobert*. From his birth in 1912 until he was a toddler, these were written on his behalf by a succession of adults employed to look after him. Clearly wishing to please her, they refer to Rachel as 'mother dear'. The *Journals* make fascinating reading, for Alasdair's upbringing seems to have been carried out according to a plan designed to shape and form his character. Thus, he was actively encouraged to be independent from a very early age and, even when he was only two years old, he was prevailed upon to play or walk outside by himself for an hour each day.

According to the *Journals*, Alasdair was fascinated by the moon. 'The moon is a great favourite of mine in every way,' he – or his proxies – wrote. When he was three, a Mr Pandit from Cawnpore drew up a horoscope for him. No one was surprised by the revelation that he would be wealthy, but Mr Pandit also predicted that he would undertake many journeys and warned that great care should be taken over his health.

In common with his younger brothers Roderic and Iain, Alasdair was indeed a sickly child. His early failure to thrive was put down to the low quality of the milk produced by local dairies, but his mother soon solved this problem: she established her own herd of Friesian cattle at Douneside. In 1923, Alastair, whose teachers noticed was not a robust child, was diagnosed with osteomyelitis in both legs. After he had undergone painful surgery, his doctors decreed that he would need a further operation. This was carried out in Aberdeen so that he could convalesce at Douneside and continue his education with the help of a tutor. The doctors told him he would make a full recovery.

While Alasdair was at home, the well-known painter, Charles Edmund Brock, was commissioned to paint the boys. When, some years later, the House of Cromar came into the ownership of the MacRobert family, the portraits were incorporated into the panelling there. Alasdair was depicted as a studious child sitting with a book on his lap, while his brothers were captured in a more informal setting outdoors in the wild.

As he grew up, Alasdair continued to be dogged by ill health. He was diagnosed with albuminuria, a condition that affects the urinary system, and was sent to recuperate in Jamaica, accompanied by a nurse and a tutor. When he was able to attend school, his reports painted a picture of an enthusiastic child who could also be highly-strung, impetuous and strong-willed. His headmaster wrote of his ten-year-old pupil:

> I am very much impressed with the boy's mental abilities – his brain is most distinctly tremendously alive ... [He is a child] with such an alert and rapid brain, who takes in so much in such profound quiet and who delivers his answers with such decision and clearness when he speaks.

He also confessed to finding Alasdair reticent and inscrutable and his personality difficult to understand. He was right in recognising his potential, for Alasdair went on to study at Trinity College Cambridge.

Alasdair's brother Roderic was born in 1915. He was given the middle name Alan, in honour of his godfather, Mac's great friend, G.B. Allan. He too, was quite a frail child. Early on, he contracted pneumonia and he suffered from emphysema and an inflamed heart, although he recovered from all these afflictions completely.

Roderic's school reports suggest that he was a diligent child interested in music: by the age of six he seems to have been an accomplished player of the violin. He studied music but he also went to St John's College Cambridge to read accountancy and estate management, presumably with a view to looking after his interests in future years.

When Iain the third son was born in 1917, Rachel's father wrote offering his congratulations or, perhaps, commiserations: 'Mama is disappointed it is not a girl.' Although he too, was not a strong child, Iain's health improved after he had his appendix removed. He studied at Grenoble University in France before he also went to Cambridge, graduating with a BA in economics in 1939.

The boys often accompanied their mother on her travels round Europe, and with her encouragement, they became able and enthusiastic sportsmen. At Douneside, they met people from many cultures and walks of life: through many idyllic summers the house was constantly buzzing with an eclectic mix of guests. The one constant in their lives was Rachel's secretary, Marjorie Ferguson, who was like a mother to the boys and kept an eye on them as they were growing up.

They all loved speed and derring-do. Alasdair, who was passionate about cars, was thrilled to attend a lecture on the production of Austin cars and planned to visit the Brooklands racing circuit. He was surely ecstatic when, in 1931, Rachel gave him permission to have a motor of his own. He became a stalwart of the Irish Motor Racing Club and competed in races at Koblenz in Germany and at Donington Park in England with varying degrees of success. His driving style, however, caused great consternation in the village and he was eventually banned from the road for dangerous driving, having also notched up four counts for speeding.

The boys spent a lot of time together enjoying their passion for cars, but they found flight, which was then in its infancy, an equally irresistible challenge. In 1935, Alasdair learned to fly with the instructors at the Upper Provinces flying club at Cawnpore, and Roderic earned his wings with the Cambridge University Air Squadron before joining the RAF Volunteer Reserve at Redhill, close to his home in Surrey. Iain followed his brother Roderic when he trained as a pilot and also took instruction in navigation and aeroplane mechanics at Cambridge. He wrote to his mother that Marshall's Flying School was government-run and used modern fighter planes. It awarded him a certificate allowing him to carry passengers in a de Havilland Fox Moth aircraft.

Probably the best fun they ever enjoyed together was a family celebration which was described by Roderic to his grandfather as 'two of the finest parties ever heard of'. Alasdair had celebrated his 21st birthday at Stanstead House, their home in Caterham in Surrey. Now it was the turn of Douneside to recognise this auspicious milestone, and on 2 August, 1933, Rachel's guests were welcomed there in spectacular fashion. The entrance to Douneside had been transformed and an arch created from purple and white heather. Over it was draped the clan tartan with the family's coat of arms in the centre. Rachel gave a luncheon for an illustrious group of guests that included Lord Aberdeen the former Viceroy of Ireland and Governor-General of Canada and their neighbour at the House of Cromar. He was eighty-seven years old but proposed the toast to Alasdair in a spirited and witty speech that showed his regard for the MacRobert family.

Rather than hire a band and the services of a Master of Ceremonies, Rachel decided to engage an entertainer of the highest calibre to regale her guests. The man she chose was William Heughan, a fine Scottish singer whose voice, which ranged from baritone to tenor, was renowned for its versatility and had given much pleasure to audiences all over the world.

Heughan was a performer of international fame, an actor and 'personality' whom Rachel had already heard sing. Born in Dalbeattie, the son of a blacksmith, he studied in London and Milan and served with the Gordon Highlanders in the First World War. A man of many and varied talents, he was one of the best pistol shots in Europe. He was also a farmer, writer, poet and cat lover. No one at the time could have suspected that this engagement was the beginning of a lifelong association with Douneside for this enigmatic character and that he would eventually become Chief Trustee and manager of the estate. His job at the birthday lunch was to entertain the guests with songs from his extensive repertoire: they ranged from folk ballads to excerpts from opera.

Afterwards the guests were taken round the estate and treated to a tour of the garden which was in full bloom. The celebrations continued into the night when the company enjoyed dinner followed by a bonfire and fireworks display which could be seen from miles around. As darkness fell, the house was floodlit, and on the driveway Venetian poles and streamers were illuminated to guide everyone home.

For the guests it was a day to remember, despite the 'incredible amount' of whisky they were said to have drunk.

The following evening, Douneside welcomed about 500 guests – tenants, estate staff and friends – who enjoyed a concert and dancing in a marquee. William Heughan was again the star performer: his singing and Roderic's playing of the violin had the audience spellbound. On behalf of those present, Lord Aberdeen presented Alasdair with a magnificent drinks cabinet. It was a night long remembered in the Howe.

Afterwards, Rachel wrote to her father to tell him it was 'touching to see how they – [the guests] worshipped me'. Roderic wrote to his grandfather: 'A really Highland atmosphere was provided by pipe music, the glow of the heather from the surrounding hills, and the sound of Doric voices.'

Alasdair now decided to devote more time to his business interests. In 1935, although he was no more enchanted with India than Rachel, he agreed to assume his responsibilities in the company that his father had worked so hard to build. Inevitably he had both supporters and detractors on the board, but eventually in 1937, at an Extraordinary General Meeting called by his mother, he was elected Chairman of the British India Corporation.

As Rachel had predicted, without Mac at the helm, the company had gone through some difficult years, thanks to the fragile political situation and the Depression. Although the British had recognised the service that Indians had rendered to the Empire during World War I by giving them more opportunities and greater autonomy in the governance of the country, they remained firmly in control. Led by Gandhi, and before him Nehru, the people of India felt they should have more say in their governance and demanded further reforms.

Alasdair found that the business was plagued with racial issues and was discredited by the Congress Party whenever its members could find an opportunity. Since Mac's death, they had successfully introduced a boycott on imports and non-Indian goods and the result was a restless workforce. To avoid being boycotted, the BIC's employees demanded that an Indian should be elected to the board which meant that the company had to be restructured. Thus the managers of each company within the BIC were appointed as managing directors with a seat on the board of the umbrella organisation. Logie Watson was appointed Chairman.

Internal wrangling saw the directors struggle for power between themselves. Thanks to this and a world economic decline, not every company within the group was operating profitably. To help improve things, Rachel agreed to delay drawing a payment due to Roderic and Iain but on condition that she remained a director and that she was kept fully informed of events. Yet although her co-directors tried to persuade her to attend meetings of the Board regularly, her dislike of India made her determined to stay away from the country. In true Mac style however, to compensate the workers for their short hours and the resultant pay cuts during these difficult times, the company agreed to reduce the rents paid by those who lived in the MacRobert *ganjs*.

There is much conflicting information about the internal wrangling that followed Mac's death, but it would appear that Robert Menzies was an ally of Rachel and Alasdair. His background was typical of those who went to work in India. He had served in the army with the Ninth Royal Scots – the 'Dandy Ninth' – before setting up in Edinburgh as a Chartered Accountant. One day, Mac walked into his office and offered him the job of Secretary and Accountant at the British India Corporation, a position he assumed at its inception. Later, he became a director and then Managing Director and consequently he alienated Logie Watson who resigned from the Company.

Menzies survived a move to oust him in the mid-1930s and went on to score a major coup for the BIC in 1946 by buying one of its rivals. He was knighted and dubbed the second King of Cawnpore, following in Mac's footsteps. He and his wife Jenny were the leading lights of society in the city during the war years.

Meanwhile, something had gone wrong with the relationship with Mac's nephew, Arthur Lilley, who at one time had been viewed as Mac's successor. He seems to have been granted a power of attorney in respect of Rachel's shares in around 1928, but Alasdair wrote in a coded message to his mother in April 1937 to 'strongly recommend granting of discharge' so that Arthur would cause no more trouble and would be 'folded out of the picture'.

Although the BIC turned the corner and became stable and profitable under his chairmanship, Alasdair became disenchanted with India and with his role. He found the number of social events he was expected to attend irksome and tedious. In his letters home to his mother, he complained that the conversation round the dinner tables seemed to be confined to gossip: matters of little interest to someone as young and energetic as Alasdair. He did however, take his appointment as Chairman of the Georgina McRobert Hospital seriously and apparently undertook his duties with enthusiasm. Mac's memorial to Georgina needed his help: it was in decline and reliant on voluntary donations to keep it operational.

Alasdair was obsessed with flying. He took lessons from the resident RAF instructor at the aerodrome at Cawnpore, and proved his efficiency at the controls. During the course of his duties as Chairman of the British India Corporation, he flew extensively throughout that country, clocking up almost 1,000 hours in his logbook. His sense of fun, his organisational skills and his meticulous attention to detail made him a formidable competitor in the Viceroy's Trophy, a round India air race that was fiercely contested.

He finished close behind the leaders and was inspired to buy his own plane, a BA Eagle. This was despite his assertion in a letter to his mother in 1935 that he had decided to learn to fly but had 'no intentions of owning an aircraft or anything like that'. He was a confident pilot and made a pioneering solo flight from Surrey to Bombay in 1937.

Alasdair toyed with the idea of erecting a hangar and building a runway at Douneside but never did so. Instead, he became a pioneer of civil aviation in India, recognising that flight would play a large part in India's future and that of the Empire. In 1936, using a generous cheque sent to him by his grandfather, he set up the Indian Aviation Development Company in partnership with Vaughan Fowler of BA Eagle Aeroplanes. This company was the first of its kind in India and offered its clients the services of pilots, mechanics and aircraft to fly anywhere in the world for business or pleasure.

Alasdair's passion for flight spilled over into the mechanical and technical side of aviation. The company also set up a 'one-stop-shop' by providing hangars and sales and services for any aircraft. They were agents too for the sale of motor cars and offered vehicles for hire, complete with driver if required. The *Aeroplane* magazine of 18 August 1937 reported that the company had been appointed aeronautical consultants to a number of Indian states and was set to develop aerodromes there.

Alasdair had been successful in convincing Indian princes of the benefits of flight and believed that the time was ripe to further develop the aviation side of his business interests. It was to prove a fatal decision. In April 1937, Alasdair had crashed his plane on take off from Turkey en route to the Coronation of King George VI but escaped with minor injuries. He was undeterred and like his brothers, fully subscribed to the words quoted at the beginning of this chapter, 'that to live a happy life, one must live a dangerous one'. As events were to prove, this love of living dangerously brought about his death.

On 1 June 1938, he was killed, along with his two passengers, in a flying accident near Luton Airport in Bedfordshire. Only a few days earlier he had arrived back in Britain and was on his way to assess some new aircraft which he hoped to use to expand his business. With him were two fellow members of the Redhill Flying Club. Eyewitness accounts suggested that as the plane came in to land it banked steeply before nose-diving to the ground. None of those aboard survived.

Alasdair was just 26 years old and the loss of her 'quiet and unassuming' first-born, the young man who had 'won the hearts and minds of all in whatever walk of life', was a body blow to Rachel. At his 21st birthday celebrations, Alastair had paid tribute to his mother who was carrying out the plans that she and his father had envisaged for Douneside. He vowed to play his part too:

> In speaking of my father who was well known to many of you, I am naturally reminded of the task that has fallen upon me to uphold the traditions associated with his name. That will be no light task but to the best of my ability, I will carry it out.

In hindsight, another speech made on the same occasion seems particularly poignant. When John McArthur of Parkhouse handed over gifts from the staff at Douneside and Melgum, he expressed the hope that they would be the first of many heirlooms, which in the course of time would record the successive comings of age of Alasdair's descendants. But it was not to be.

Rachel later sent a simple message from Stanstead House to those who had sent expressions of sympathy:

> Douneside and Cromar have lost a weel-loved laird and Scotland a son of brilliant promise.

Alasdair was cremated at Golders Green in London on 4 June 1938. The service was conducted by the Reverend H.W. Beck, vicar of Grenhill, Ruislip. His mother's friend Maria Ogilvie Gordon, by then elevated to a Dame, Logie Watson's wife and daughter, Sir Robert Menzies and John McCaw the Douneside estate manager were among those present at the funeral. On 5 June the Reverend William Low preached in Tarland Church. 'The great robber Death,' He said, 'Has stretched out his shadowy arm and stolen this young life so rich in promise. ... We have rejoiced with those who rejoiced, surely we must weep with those who wept'.

Rachel decided that Alasdair's ashes should be buried in a cairn designed by William Heughan in the garden of Alastrean House, the mansion which had become the property of the MacRoberts and a base for the boys when they were at home in Aberdeenshire. In August 1938, Rachel wrote to Roderic that she was well pleased with his design of the cairn and with the workmanship of Mr Leslie the builder, who hailed from Torphins. She also took advice from a Mr Peter, who suggested that she should make the cairn larger than she had at first intended:

'We are building for all time and must have room for future generations,' he said.

The Cairn was dedicated by the Reverend William Low on 5 January 1939 and there Alasdair's ashes found their resting place. Its four bronze panels are inscribed with the words:

| The day ends here | the night comes on |
| But sunset here | is elsewhere dawn. |

Alasdair left estate in England worth £2,461: around £90,000 in today's money.

In memory of Alasdair, BIC's shareholders were encouraged to endow a ward in his name at the Georgina McRobert Memorial Hospital in Cawnpore in the hope that it would become the best equipped, resourced and modern facility in Central India as his father had always intended. The family led the way: his brothers donated 500 preference shares, and Rachel, who for some time had been sending funds to help offset the deficit, made her own contribution. With these funds the hospital was at last in a position to undertake major repairs and install such basic facilities as running water and washbasins in the outpatients' department.

Sir Robert Menzies, who was also a Governor of the Board at the Hospital wrote expressing its thanks that with her financial support the hospital now boasted a modern operating theatre. It had also been able to install an ever-welcome cooling plant, air conditioners, fans and a powerful lighting system.

Rachel had got her wish for Sir Robert added,

'I have pleasure in confirming that the revenue from this additional endowment will cover the cost of maintaining one ward and that such ward will be known henceforth as the Sir Alasdair Workman MacRobert Memorial Ward.'

Meanwhile, the storm clouds of war were gathering. Roderic, who was studying music at the Mozarteum in Salzburg, recorded his observations of the mood in Austria just before the hostilities began. He wrote:

> I consider that all the recent behaviour (of the Nazis) is high handed, unreasonable and completely unworthy of modern civilization. I'd rather live in Russia.

He was already weary of hearing people condemn Hitler: 'He must soon die a horrid death by telepathy,' He said.

Roderic now became the third Baronet of Cawnpore and Cromar, although only a few years had passed since Mac had been given the title. He wanted to go to India to carry on the Indian Aviation Development Company in his brother's footsteps, but Rachel dissuaded him. She argued, rather unkindly, that Alasdair's success there had been due to his personality and to his position as Chairman of the British India Corporation.

Earlier that year, 1938, Roderic had joined the RAF. He had been commissioned as a pilot officer and sent to a Service Flying School in Egypt. Later, after joining a bomber squadron in Palestine with the rank of Acting Flight Lieutenant his deeds during the Arab revolt earned him the Palestine medal. He was clearly held in high regard. He was appointed adjutant to Air Vice Marshall Sir Arthur Harris, the Air Officer commanding RAF Palestine and Transjordan, accompanying him to England just before the war. Later when war threatened, he was posted back to the Middle East then appointed Personal Assistant to Air Vice Marshall Reid, Air Officer commanding Aden.

He became frustrated by his largely administrative role where his duties included bringing the squadron history up-to-date. But the Iraqi revolt that lasted from 2 May 1941 until 31st of that month heralded a move to command a detachment of a Hurricane Squadron. He was a popular figure at the base and his leadership in ground-strafing operations in support of the land army earned him the respect of his fellow officers and men. He was soon regarded as a veteran amongst Middle East pilots.

On 22 May 1941, Roderic led a fighter attack on the Mosul air base in Iraq, when many Junkers and Messerschmitts of the enemy's were destroyed or put out of action. The pilot of the other Hurricane fighter involved in the raid described how Roderic had made a daring swoop:

> When we arrived over Mosul, MacRobert dived down to make an attack. Almost at once, his fire set alight two lorries laden with petrol. These went up with a dickens of a flash. Then I came down and we both strafed hangars and aircraft on the ground. I saw MacRobert come down in a second dive and turn away after the attack, but after that, I never saw him again. Although we are not certain of this, we think he must have been shot down on the way back.

Their base was a long haul from their target and involved flying the long range Hurricanes over desert country. The pilot continued:

> Our raid was made primarily against Junkers 52s and ME109s, as well

as Iraqi rebel aircraft on the aerodrome. We were also after German ground personnel and anti aircraft gun positions. Only when the revolt was over did we find out how successful the raid had been. Large numbers of Junkers and Messerschmitts were found riddled with machine-gun bullets and we also learned that some German pilots were killed by MacRobert in that daring dive, when he went headlong for the enemy.

When she heard the news of Roderic's death, Rachel said:

I am proud to think he did his duty, and carried out so well the spirit of our family motto – Virtutis Gloria Merce [Glory is the reward of valour].

His remains were later recovered and he is buried in Mosul War Cemetery.

Iain now became the fourth Baronet, only some 20 years since the title was first created for his father.

When war broke out in 1939, he had joined the RAF voluntary reserve and in 1940 was commissioned as a Pilot Officer. After a spell at the School of General Reconnaissance, he was posted to coastal command at Thorganby near Stockton. He took part in North Sea patrols and his quiet and unassuming manner, akin to his brother Roderic's, earned him the respect of officers and men.

He flew 25 operational flights escorting convoys along the east coast and making daylight reconnoitres over Denmark and Norway.

On 30 June, just a few weeks after Roderic was posted missing and after he had returned from Douneside where had had gone to comfort his mother, Iain and his crew joined other aircraft in the search for the men of a bomber believed ditched in the North Sea off Flamborough Head.

The search had been going on for two days, and that Saturday morning, Iain took off in one of the better Blenheims. The plane was not carrying bombs and, as was normal, he maintained radio silence.

Two dinghies with ten men aboard were rescued, but at landing time Iain had not returned. His Flight Commander took off in a fruitless search for him. A massive search took place the next day but this also failed to locate any trace of the aircraft. Neither plane nor crew was ever found.

It was thought unlikely that pilot error, a fuel shortage or engine failure was the cause of Iain's disappearance. The most plausible theory was that enemy fighters operating from the Dutch coast had come out of the sun and shot him down.

His Flight Commander Peter Vaux told Rachel that Iain had been the best all-round pilot in the Squadron and that he had been in line for early promotion. He added:

> His keenness and courage when going on operational flights was the highest I have ever seen – he never faltered or hesitated and we all admired him.

While Iain's body was never recovered his name is remembered on the Air Forces Memorial at Runnymede, four miles from Windsor, which commemorates the names of over 20,000 airmen lost in World War II and who have no known grave.

Peter Vaux added:

> I am terribly grieved to hear of Mac's (Iain was known as Mac in the squadron) two brothers. It must make this last blow so hard to bear.

Rachel was now without any close family. Her parents had also died and she had lost all three sons in their prime and within such a short space of time. But her spirit proved dauntless and her own war campaign was just beginning.

The boys growing up at Douneside.

Left to right:
Roderic, Iain and Alasdair aged 5, 4 and 8.
(The MacRobert Trust)

A proud and happy mother. Rachel with her sons Alasdair, Roderic and Iain.
(Aberdeen Journals Ltd)

*Celebrating Alasdair's 21st birthday
at Douneside is guest of honour
Lord Aberdeen pictured with
Alasdair and his mother.*
(Aberdeen Journals Ltd)

Flying Officer Peter Boggis gives the 'thumbs up' sign.
(The MacRobert Trust)

Stirling Bombers. Return of the MacRobert's Reply by Charles Edward Cundall, 1942.
(RAF Museum/National Museum of Scotland)

"We'll do our job – –if you'll do yours"

The crew of the bomber plane "MacRobert's Reply" all ready to take off for a raid over enemy territory

A propaganda poster issued by the UK Government.

Pooled Resources

THESE factories pictured here, have pooled their vast resources. ¶ Working hand in hand they have so perfected their products and reduced manufacturing costs that to-day their goods represent the very highest quality at prices that are remarkably low. ¶ It will pay you to buy their products, sold under the following Trade Names:—

LAL-IMLI PURE WOOL
EVERYTHING IN WOOL

N.W.T
EVERYTHING IN LEATHER

Kakomi Cawnpore
EVERYTHING IN COTTON

Dhariwal
LONG LIFE WOOL WEAR

THE EMPIRE ENGINEERING CO.
ENGINEERING REQUIREMENTS

FLEX
FOOT WEAR

Address all communications to the Branch concerned

The **BRITISH INDIA CORPORATION LTD.**
CAWNPORE

The British India Company advertises its wares in the 1930s

*The many faces of Rachel
– the landowner.*
(The MacRobert Trust)

*The many faces of Rachel
– the scientist*
(The MacRobert Trust)

Rachel takes time to enjoy the beautiful garden she created.
(The MacRobert Trust)

The many faces of Rachel – the gardener.
(The MacRobert Trust)

Rachel's Friesian cattle. She made her first purchases to provide
baby Alasdair with quality milk.
(The MacRobert Trust)

The many faces of
Rachel – the farmer.
(The MacRobert Trust)

When building up her fold of Highland cattle, Rachel used her scientific expertise to research the bloodlines she wished to purchase.
(The MacRobert Trust)

Emor of Derculich, one of the most influential bulls in Rachel's Aberdeen Angus herd.
(Aberdeen Journals Ltd)

Remormon of Douneside makes TV history – but Rachel died the next day.
(Aberdeen Journals Ltd)

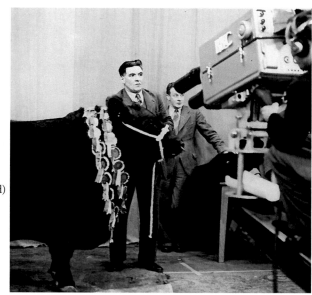

The memorial to the MacRobert boys above the door at Alastrean House.
(The MacRobert Trust)

Inspirational and evocative textile wall hanging, one of three which hang at Rachel House, Kinross depicting the MacRobert story.
(Marianne More-Gordon)

IN THE HOUR OF PERIL
LADY RACHEL WORKMAN
MACROBERT
EARNED THE GRATITUDE
OF THE BRITISH NATIONS
SUSTAINING THE VALOUR OF
THE ROYAL AIR FORCE
AND FORTIFYING THE CAUSE
OF FREEDOM
BY THE GIFT OF
BOMBER AIRCRAFT
They shall mount up with wings as eagles.
Issued by the Ministry of Aircraft Production
1942

*The Plaque given to Rachel
in Recognition of her generosity
to the war effort*
(The Martin R. Ford Jones Collection)

*The Headstone which marks
Lady MacRoberts final resting
place at Douneside*
(The Martin R. Ford Jones Collection)

CHAPTER 15

Godmother To The RAF

The best of good luck boys, always, and whenever and wherever you go. I know you will strike hard, sharp, and straight to the mark. That is the only language the enemy understands. My thoughts and thousands of other mothers are with you, and we are truly grateful to all concerned. Also thanks to those of you who have the care of my 'Reply' and prepare her for her flights. May the blows you strike bring us nearer victory. God bless you all.

With these words Rachel honoured her dead sons. But she also took action.

During Iain's last leave from the RAF, the City of Aberdeen had staged a Spitfire week to raise money to provide planes for the war effort. Iain had suggested to his mother that she might like to provide a bomber, and on 31 July 1941 she sent a cheque for £25,000 to Sir Archibald Sinclair, Secretary of State for Air.

The letter that accompanied this extraordinarily generous gift of around £700,000 in today's money revealed not only Rachel's grief but also her indomitable spirit. she wrote:

> It is my wish to make a mother's immediate reply, 'in the way that I know would also be my boys' reply – attacking, striking sharply, straight to the mark – the gift of £25,000 – to buy a bomber to carry on their work in the most effective way. This expresses my reaction on receiving the news about my sons.

> I am proud to read what you say about their work. I never doubted but that they would do their duty.

> They would be glad that their mother replied for them, and helped to strike a blow at the enemy. So I feel that a suitable name for the bomber would be 'MacRobert's Reply'. Might it carry the MacRobert Crest, or simply our Badge – a frond of bracken and an Indian Rose crossed?

Let it be used where it is most needed. May good fortune go with those who fly it.

I have no more sons to wear the Badge, or carry it in the fight. If I had ten sons, I know they would all have followed that line of duty. It is with a mother's pride that I enclose my cheque for £25,000 – and with it goes my sympathy to those mothers who have also lost sons, and gratitude to all other mothers whose sons so gallantly carry on the fight.'

Sir Archibald Sinclair's reply to Lady Rachel confirmed the close link between the family and the RAF:

MacRobert's Reply will proudly bear with it into action the crest of a family which has given so much to Britain. Your pride and sorrow are shared by your sons' comrades in the Royal Air Force. They knew their worth who shared their perils, but not their glorious end.

Those whose duty it will be to fly the MacRobert's Reply against the enemy, will have to guide them the shining example of Roderic and Iain, whose glory, in the words of the motto of their Clan, 'is the reward of valour'.

The opening words of this chapter come from Rachel's message to the crew of the first Shorts Stirling, serial N6086 and coded LS-F, when it was officially handed over to XV Squadron at RAF Wyton in Cambridgeshire.

At the time, the Stirling was the world's largest working bomber, the first with four engines to enter service with the RAF. Of extremely robust construction, the Stirling had a reputation for being able to reach its home base even after taking direct hits by flak, but its speed was what made it such a superb weapon of war. Such was its manoeuvrability that, when empty of its bombs, it could engage, chase and shoot down enemy fighters with ease. It was also highly efficient: a Stirling was capable of carrying as many bombs as three or four Wellingtons, but required only seven men to man it in comparison with six for each Wellington.

The pilot chosen for the 'Reply' was Flying Officer Peter Boggis: for him it was the beginning of a life-long association with the MacRoberts. Sixty-two years later, in March 2003, he unveiled a bronze sculpture of the plane at Douneside. Rachel and his wife Kay also became friends: Kay served as a Trustee of the MacRobert Trust for forty-one years.

The aircraft was deployed on active service from October 1941 until January 1942, flying twelve operational sorties. The longest was to attack the Skoda factory at Pilsen in Czechoslovakia, but perhaps its most memorable mission was a raid on Brest Harbour in France in December 1941 where two enemy ships, *Scharnhorst* and *Gneisenau*, were under repair in dry dock. This attack, in broad daylight and in the face of ferocious defensive action by the Germans, earned Peter Boggis the DFC

Boggis reported:

> We bombed from 14,000 feet at 12.37 hours. Bursts of 250lb bombs in the middle of the stick believed seen just short of the dry dock. Black smoke was also rising from the Gneisenau after the bombing. We were attacked by 3 Me109s, one of which is claimed as damaged.

It was a successful raid. The accuracy of the bombing left the ships billowing black smoke in the air.

Many years later, Boggis's memories of the day were still fresh:

> As soon as we completed our bombing run we put our nose down and headed for the Channel. Once back over the sea and flown almost to sea level in case there were still fighters about, our rear gunner suddenly reported a formation of six aircraft approaching from behind.

They were Halifaxes also returning from the Brest raid and flying low to gain speed.

> They were a welcome sight. They opened up their formation in invitation and gratefully we climbed and were enfolded in their midst. We returned in grand style.

The first MacRobert's Reply came to a sorry end soon after. Peter had completed two tours of duty and had moved on to become an instructor. The Stirling was deployed to Lossiemouth to take part in a mission code-named 'Operation Oiled', in search of the *Tirpitz* which was moored in Trondheim Fjord, partly camouflaged. This great battleship, the pride of the Baltic fleet, had survived numerous raids over the years. She was the scourge of the convoys and a painful thorn in the side of the Allies.

After delays due to bad weather, the planes left Lossiemouth, only to be diverted to Peterhead because of ice and snow. On take-off the next morning, MacRobert's Reply slid off the runway and collided with a Spitfire. Badly damaged, she was put on a low loader and transported back to base where ground crew transferred the panels carrying her name to another Stirling bomber – W7531.

'Operation Oiled' had to be abandoned, but the hunt for the *Tirpitz* went on. The story of how she was finally found and destroyed also has a MacRobert connection.

On 12 July 1944, Flight Lieutenant Frank Dodd and his navigator flew to the Norwegian Coast in search of German vessels. En route, the top cover of their aircraft blew off, but they carried on to complete their journey without it and in freezing conditions. Since their codebooks had blown out of the open hatch, they could not radio back to base. Despite these desperate conditions, Dodd and his navigator succeeded in identifying, locating, and photographing the *Tirpitz*.

Their bravery, on a journey that had taken eight hours and covered 2,300 miles, was recognised by the award of the Distinguished Service Order (DSO) to Dodd, and of the Distinguished Flying Medal (DFM) to his navigator Eric Hill.

The *Tirpitz* survived many raids until, on 12 November 1944, she was attacked by 32 Lancaster Bombers from RAF Coningsby in 'Operation Catechism.' Two 'Tallboy' bombs hit her on the port side amidships and she capsized. Three months later, Dodd and Hill flew the RAF's last reconnaissance operation to the northern Arctic to photograph *Tirpitz* lying partially submerged in the bay of Håkøybotn near Tromsø. The flight took more than ten hours, and covered more than 3,000 miles, and was reputedly the longest photographic reconnaissance flight of the whole war. For this epic sortie, both men were awarded the Distinguished Flying Cross (DFC).

Frank Dodd ended his distinguished career as an Air Vice-Marshal and when he retired from the RAF worked as the Administrator of the MacRobert Trusts from 1974 to 1985.

Meanwhile, in May 1942, the new 'MacRobert's Reply' was sent to bomb mining operations in Scandinavia. One of its engines was hit by flak from ships in the Baltic and the plane was finally brought down by ground defences and crashed in the forest at Galsklint on the island of Funen in Denmark. Of the crew, only Sergeant Duncan Jeffs, the mid-upper gunner survived. He was thrown clear of the aircraft and later taken prisoner by the Germans.

The name 'MacRobert's Reply' was not to grace the fuselage of an aircraft again for the next forty years. Then, at a ceremony in 1982, the by now Squadron Leader Boggis proudly unveiled the frond of bracken and the Indian rose on a new MacRobert's Reply, a Buccaneer 'XT287', coded F. Since then, every aircraft that is coded 'F' with XV Squadron proudly carries the name.

The gift of the Stirling bomber was not the only gesture Rachel made in memory of her sons. By 1942, inspired by the fortitude of the Russians in the defence of their country, she decided to mark her admiration by donating £20,000 (around £500,000 in today's money) for the purchase of four Hurricane fighters. Again, she wrote to Sir Archibald Sinclair at the Air Ministry:

The whole world has been astonished at the magnificent resistance of the Russian people. They have not counted the cost. The fighting qualities of their men and women, united in their hearts and minds, strong in their unity, are beyond what the world might have considered their utmost or possible. The hardest continuous blows could not break them. No mere words can express my admiration for what has been done and is being done under the magnificent and inspired leadership of Stalin. Hitler can never destroy such spirit and people any more than they can destroy us. If we all do our very utmost to help, now the Allied victory may not be so far off.

May this message reach Russia and her heroic women, the mothers, who, like myself, have proudly given their sons, their all. I cannot go and be a pilot myself. Had I been a man, I, too, would have flown on such service, but I wish to give a fighter, to be named 'MacRobert's Salute to Russia – The Lady' to let them know we are with them to the very end – both materially and spiritually – until the victory has been won and freedom lives again...

The other three fighters were to be named 'Sir Alasdair', 'Sir Roderic' and 'Sir Iain'. She continued:

As our family has long been associated with India, it is right that the name should be on the front nearest to India where our RAF would be helping Russia. I feel that my son, Sir Roderic, when he fell attacking the German planes at Mosul, did something to upset their plans at that time. Somewhere in the Middle East, our forces might be closely associated with the Russians in fighting and defeating the common enemy. So there, where he fell, may there be three more fighters to join in the fray, bearing the MacRobert name.

May this message reach Russia and her heroic women. I salute the indomitable heart of such a country, such women – such mothers who, like myself, have proudly given their sons, their all.

On 20 March 1942, the *Evening Telegraph* and other newspapers throughout the land carried a piece headed 'Russian Women's Thanks to Lady MacRobert': Her letter evoked a response from a committee of Russian women who wrote from Moscow:

Your letter has found a response in the heart of every Soviet woman. For the sake of victory over the evil genius of humanity – Fascism – you have sacrificed three sons. Maternal feelings are the same everywhere. We know what it means to lose three sons. This turns the bravest hearts to stone but you have as defiant a heart as the hearts of the Soviet women who you praise. You prefer to turn your enemies into stone. Your sons are dead but you are sending fighters into the skies which they conquered so that other sons and their mothers will be able to live in a liberated world.

Rachel knew what a difference a successful foray by the Germans into Iraq would make to the outcome of the war: they had to be prevented from capturing its oilfields and from opening up a route into India to link up with the Japanese, who were advancing from the other side.

The Hawker Hurricanes Mark 11C were allocated to the Russian Air Regiment which flew with Roderic's old 94 squadron based in the Western

Desert. A British Pathé newsreel of the handing-over ceremony at El Gamil in Egypt on 19 September 1942 shows the young men of the squadron giving a rousing three cheers for their benefactor. For Rachel, this must have been a poignant reminder of her own lost sons.

In his speech at the ceremony, Air Vice Marshal Wilfred McClaughry said it should be the aim of all of those there that day to show the spirit and courage and superlative heroism of 'this brave mother' who saw the spirit of her sons carrying on the fight. The MacRobert name, he added, would live on in these acts of generosity and support.

Alasdair made an indirect contribution to the war effort. He had registered an Eagle 3-seater racing aircraft as G-AEFZ in April 1936. After his death it was sold on, until in 1941 it was pressed into service with the RAF where it was used for communications duties at Wattisham in Suffolk. Later it was transferred to Northolt and Leuchars, but when its undercarriage collapsed at Turnhouse in July 1943, the plane was deemed beyond repair.

Buying aircraft for the RAF was not Rachel's only way of supporting Britain's fighting forces: she also devoted much of her time and energy to travelling the country encouraging others to help. Although she admitted to being uneasy about speaking in public, her passion for the cause overcame this and she embarked on a whirl of morale-boosting engagements.

'Remember how your freedom has been won. This heritage must be protected. Teachers must foster the right spirit in schools. No one must forget at what a cost was purchased this freedom and particularly remember always how the flower of our youth did their duty even to the utmost sacrifice. Remember their spirit and their unselfishness. They succeeded in stemming the tide of destruction and winning the victory; because they were well led – had been well trained, and were well able to do their best. We all must keep faith with them.'

Ten years later, these words quoted from one of Rachel's rallying calls was repeated by her confidant and factotum William Heughan to remind those gathered for the opening of the MacRobert Hall in Tarland of her spirit and tenacity.

Reports in almost every newspaper in the land told of her losses and her fortitude, and she was soon in demand as a speaker at rallies. The Government produced a propaganda poster depicting 'MacRobert's Reply' and her crew: its caption read, 'We'll do our job – if you'll do yours.'

As Rachel became a household name, William Heughan found himself writing more and more speeches and replying to the huge volume of letters that flooded in from admirers all over the world.

The Salvation Army asked her to speak in a broadcast, 'The Week's Good Cause', in aid of their Centres where they provided 'spiritual strength and physical comfort to alleviate stress and loneliness.'

Her speeches were met with ovations wherever she spoke. In one, she hailed the courage of the women of Malta during the fight for control of the Mediterranean and the siege of that strategically important island. Her attacks on the Nazis and the way they treated the people of the countries they had invaded were relentless and heartfelt. Victory, she said, would 'come through the blood of heroes and fighters.'

In another speech, she commended the ship-workers on the Clyde whose efforts could 'make all the difference between a long struggle and early and complete victory'.

In May 1943, when austerity measures were in full force in Britain, the inauguration ceremony of 'Wings for Victory Week' brought a welcome touch of carnival to Glasgow. Thousands of people turned out to hear her speak and to support the campaign which aimed to raise £13,500,000 nationally.

Rachel was greeted warmly by the crowd as she urged them to 'strike hard for all you hold dear, for home and country.' 'Hitler,' she proclaimed, 'must not only be brought to account but must surrender and be punished. He had to be defeated and his power destroyed.

'We must bear the price paid for freedom and supply more wings with which to do it,' she said. 'Everyone has their bit to play in addition to those who fight in the air and on land and on sea. Those in the fields, down mines, in factories and shipyards can play their part to preserve our freedom. Glasgow could lead the way.'

At the 'Wings for Victory' day, she was allowed to experience what Roderic would have felt in the cockpit of his plane when she sat at the controls of a Link Trainer simulator.

The parade of 2,000 RAF, WAAF and ATC personnel was dominated by a Lancaster bomber, 'P for Peter', which, along with a Hurricane fighter, took pride of place in the city's George Square.

When Rachel spoke the words 'Wings for Victory', more than 1,000 pigeons were released. Later in the ceremony, 101 more took to the air as a tribute to her.

'Make no mistake about it. The enemy knows how hard the RAF can strike, and is striking. Glasgow has its opportunity now to make the blow even harder.'

She exhorted Glaswegians to make their campaign so successful that Hitler would know what the city thought of him and his gang, and added 'And he will know.' The response was rousing cheers: Glasgow was in fighting mood that day – fighting against Hitler that is.

Thanks to the efforts of the organisers and the enthusiasm and passion of the speakers at similar events throughout the country, the 'Wings for Victory' campaign exceeded its target.

In 1945, Rachel founded the MacRobert Reply Association, a scheme for the betterment of members of youth organisations in Scotland. While supporting the forces, especially those who fought in the air, she also recognised that those injured on active service or traumatised from being incarcerated in Prisoner of War camps needed to recuperate in peaceful surroundings.

She knew – she owned exactly the right place: Alastrean House, in Tarland. She had intended it to be a base for her sons when they came home to the Howe of Cromar – but she had no use for it now. She put the house at the disposal of the RAF to be used as a rest home for airmen where, surrounded by peace and security, their minds and bodies could recover from the trauma of combat and all the horrors of war.

CHAPTER 16

Ladies at Loggerheads

3 September, 1934. We had a little gathering of the household for the morning service on the wireless. I said a few words of thanks to all, then a prayer for future blessing on this house.

Lady Aberdeen's diary entry was the last she wrote from the House of Cromar, her beloved home for almost thirty years.

Douneside occupies an idyllic spot, commanding breathtaking views over the saucer-shaped valley of the Howe of Cromar to the Deeside hills where Lochnagar towers to the west. Below it, on the edge of Tarland stood the House of Cromar, once the home of the Marquess and Marchioness of Aberdeen and Temair. This was the place that Rachel offered as a rest and recuperation home for RAF personnel, but not before the transfer of ownership had caused some animosity between her and Lady Aberdeen. With the passing of time it is hard to disentangle the true story.

In 1729 the Cromar estate was bought by William, second Earl of Aberdeen, from John Coutts of Auchtercoull. At one time it had extended almost to the River Dee and encompassed the Muir of Dinnet. Despite the constant need to drain the land, the fields were fine and fertile. Lady Aberdeen though was disappointed to discover soon after she was married that the only accommodation for the family was Tarland Lodge, a small farmhouse used by the Aberdeens during the shooting season.

Both Lady Aberdeen and her husband John Campbell Gordon, seventh Earl of Aberdeen, were dynamic characters who did not shrink from making changes where they were needed. Lord Aberdeen had a distinguished career: he was influential in Liberal politics and served as Governor General of Canada, Lord Lieutenant of Ireland, and Lord High Commissioner of the Church of Scotland.

Tarland Lodge was patently unsuitable as a home for a couple of their standing. They chose a site nearby which would accommodate a much larger house that they could fill with their distinguished friends. In 1879, Ishbel asked her father to stop by on his way to Guisachan, his highland estate, to advise her on a design. He recommended that 'the villa style would suit better than castle'.

The plan lay dormant for another twenty years: the Aberdeens were busy at Haddo House, their family seat fifty miles away across the county, and their diplomatic duties took them away on long postings overseas. When the House of Cromar was finally built in 1905 they felt it had been worth the wait.

Traditionally, the occupants of Aberdeenshire's 'big hooses' enjoyed the privacy of mansions surrounded by verdant parkland, mature trees, and manicured lawns and guarded by gate houses and lodges situated at the entrances to the policies. The House of Cromar was different: it was carefully positioned to take in a magnificent open vista and was, in consequence, less enclosed. From its many windows looking out across the valley to the foothills of the Cairngorms, the Aberdeens could observe the activities of their farming neighbours and see the smoke curling from the chimneys of the houses in Tarland. Unlike most of their peers who would summon a carriage or a car to convey them on their outings, this energetic couple preferred to stroll down to the village where their relaxed and easy manners and genuine interest in the folk there endeared them to the community.

Visitors to the House of Cromar took great pleasure in its walled garden, herbaceous border and woodland walk. The house itself was built of the pink local granite and Ishbel had a formal Italian rose garden laid out to go with it. She never tired of watching the birds that came to drink from the fountain outside her room. A pergola and the sundial stood in the middle of a lawn shaped like a double heart: for 'We Twa', as the couple liked to call themselves, this was a happy home, a haven after years of travel.

Ishbel loved gardens, and this one in particular. In 1931 she helped to found Scotland's Gardens Scheme, a still thriving charity. She wanted to raise money for District Nurses whose work was vital to the wellbeing of every local community. So great was the success of the scheme, which allowed the public to see normally inaccessible gardens on payment of a 'voluntary contribution', that the nurses' pensions were doubled to 20 pounds per year.

Among the guests who enjoyed the hospitality of the Aberdeens was Queen Mary. She made her first visit as Princess of Wales in 1907, and thereafter ensured that her annual holiday at Balmoral included a visit to the House of Cromar. In later years, the Duchess of York, who became Queen when her husband succeeded to the throne as George VI, also used to drop by with the young Princess Elizabeth and Princess Margaret. They followed a tradition established by Queen Mary of planting a tree in the grounds.

Lady Aberdeen was a great social reformer, a woman of boundless energy who had spent a lifetime carrying out good works. Her parents were horrified when, as a young woman, she ventured into some of the seediest parts of London to help rescue and rehabilitate prostitutes. After her marriage, she devoted her time to working tirelessly for numerous charities and initiatives throughout the world. She served as President of the International Council for Women for 40 years and founded what is still one of Canada's most important social organisations, the Victorian Order of Nurses. In Ireland, she led a campaign to eradicate tuberculosis and set up the Woman's National Health Association there. She was also President of the Irish Industries Association, helping the country's craftsmen and women to find export markets for their wares. She was a lifelong Liberal and the country's leading politicians flocked to her salons.

Home for her was Aberdeenshire, where her husband served as Lord Lieutenant for more than 40 years, and she continued her charity work there. As President of the County of Aberdeen branch of the British Red Cross Society, she took a particular interest in the children of Tarland School who became members of the Junior Red Cross Society. Before the establishment of the National Health Service, the couple encouraged the community to contribute to the 'penny a week' scheme which helped to fund the local district nurse.

She was a member of the executive committee of the Aberdeen County Nursing Association and in 1915, during World War I, the Aberdeens offered the Lodge as an Auxiliary Hospital. This was very much a community enterprise, supervised by the Tarland Red Cross Committee and staffed by the local physician Dr Hector, a matron, a resident nurse, and helpers recruited from the members of the local Women's Voluntary Aid Detachment.

The community rallied round and followed their Laird's example by donating funds and produce that was collected from the surrounding area. The Aberdeens provided the services of a housekeeper and cook, and they placed their motor car at the disposal of those who wished to worship at the Episcopal or Roman Catholic churches in Aboyne. They were also happy for other people to use the grounds at the House of Cromar: the patients at the hospital were very appreciative of the tennis and croquet courts – and also the golf course.

The wounded soldiers came from all over the country and from many regiments, including the Scots Guards, the Gordon Highlanders, the Royal Dublin Fusiliers, the West Kent Regiment and the Durham Light Infantry. The list of the injuries they had sustained reflected the horrors of the First World War. Some patients were suffering both physically and mentally from wounds inflicted during the retreat from Mons. One had fought in the trenches at Ypres for twenty-eight days, while others had been gassed there. Others had been wounded and suffered frostbite at Neuve Chapelle. There were cases of malaria, of pleurisy, of deafness caused by the thunder of guns and exploding shells: thus the reality of war and its pain and cost came to the Howe of Cromar.

Although Lady Aberdeen's schemes, of which there were many, were for the betterment of mankind, they were mostly funded from the Aberdeens' private purse. And when Lord Aberdeen's various public duties such as his role as Lord High Commissioner of the Church of Scotland led to his spending much more than his expense accounts allowed he had to foot the bill. His financial troubles were exacerbated by bonds on the Cromar estate. He took out further loans and in 1889, as his problems multiplied, he set up a trust and granted it a conveyance over the estate. Two trustees from a firm of Chartered Accountants in Edinburgh were appointed to help him look after their affairs. Before they left for Canada in 1893, the Aberdeens hosted a dinner for their tenants in a marquee at the House of Cromar, where they warned them of their predicament. Lord Aberdeen promised that they would try to avoid selling the Cromar estate piecemeal and that he would try to hold out until a satisfactory offer was made for the lands as a whole, even if there was no prospect of one in the immediate future. No offer ever materialised, and although they did sell some portions of land, the bonds still could not be cleared.

A second Trust was set up in 1916, and as the effects of the war grew worse, Lord Aberdeen was forced to sell outlying parts of his Haddo Estate. The only way to protect its fine mansion house and surrounding acreage was to hand them over to his son in 1920. This left the House of Cromar as their only home.

Further storm clouds were looming. The cost of running the Cromar Estate outweighed the rental income and there were no longer any reserves to meet the deficit. Gradually more land had to be sold off and a deal was done with their neighbour, Mac. In 1915, he agreed to meet the deficit run up by the estate, and three years later he bought a small parcel of land to be held in trust for Alasdair. The following year he undertook to pay off a debt of £44,850 in return for the remaining lands being held in trust. Alasdair was again its beneficiary. He also continued to meet the annual deficit of the estate which amounted to £1,900 and increased to £2,670 in 1922. The deal allowed the Aberdeens to remain as tenants of the property until the death of the second of the couple.

The decline in the Aberdeen's' financial situation continued. Without her husband knowing, Lady Aberdeen volunteered to move out after he died if he predeceased her in return for Mac agreeing to increase his contribution. The MacRoberts might then be able to take over the House of Cromar at a much earlier date.

As part of the agreement, an inventory of the contents of the House of Cromar and Tarland Lodge had to be drawn up. Letters flew between the families and their lawyers. Mac maintained that the fine paintings, furniture and artefacts in the houses were of great value, but Lady Aberdeen seems to have complicated matters by refusing to accept that the house was, in effect, being sold rather than let. She gave numerous excuses for wanting to keep many of the contents: some belonged elsewhere and were merely being stored at Cromar; some belonged to Lady Pentland and yet others to her grandchildren. Then there were things that had been owned by her mother, and the paintings in particular, were 'all most personal'. Eventually, though, an agreement was reached.

Over the years, relations between the families appeared to be cordial. In her book, *A Bonnie Fechter*, the Aberdeens' daughter, Lady Marjorie Pentland, who had socialised with Mac in India when her husband was governor of Madras, wrote that Georgina and her mother had been fond of each other. The two had much in common, not least their concern for those less fortunate than themselves. Lady Aberdeen was a constant visitor to Douneside when Georgina lay ill, and Mac never forgot her kindness. When Lady Aberdeen wrote to Rachel to express her shock and sympathy on hearing of Mac's death she said: 'If we can be of any use please command our services.' However, when Lord Aberdeen died at the age of eighty-seven, Rachel insisted on sticking to the terms of the agreement and refused to allow the grieving widow to stay on, despite her pleas.

Rachel also wanted the transfer of ownership made public immediately. The facts were duly laid out in an article in the *Scotsman* newspaper on 13 April 1934:

Estate of Cromar Passes to MacRobert Trustees;

Lady Aberdeen's Letter

We are authorised to state that by an arrangement made between the late Marquis of Aberdeen and Temair and the late Sir Alexander MacRobert, Bart., the Estate of Cromar now passes from the Trustees of the Estate of Cromar, and will be held in future by the MacRobert Trustees of Douneside and Melgum.

Farewell to Tenants

The Dowager Marchioness of Aberdeen and Temair said 'goodbye' to the tenants on the Estate of Cromar in a letter to each tenant dated April 11, which reads as follows:-

For sometime before his death, your late laird, the Marquis of Aberdeen and Temair, was considering the desirability of writing a letter of farewell to the Cromar tenants which could be delivered to them after he had passed away. But he finally decided to entrust this duty to me.

He wished you to receive a personal intimation from himself as to the arrangements he had made for the future of the estate.

For some considerable time he had realized that it was not possible for him or his successors to carry on the estate, owing to increase of taxation and other burdens.

He wished you to know that his original intention in building the House Of Cromar was to provide a home for me when he was called away, as he was always so sure that I would survive him. But when necessity arose for the Haddo House estate to be transferred to his son, we naturally desired to live amongst 'oor ain folk' in the Howe of Cromar.

This was only rendered possible by a friendly and generous arrangement with the late Sir Alexander MacRobert Bart., by virtue of which Lord Aberdeen and I were able to live amongst you in this lovely home amidst the much loved Deeside hills during the last fourteen years. Under that arrangement the estate now falls to be handed over to Sir Alexander or his heirs.

These have been happy years for us both, and the kindness of tenants and neighbours has greatly conduced to that happiness.

Lord Aberdeen felt that in transferring the property which had been in the possession of his family during more than 250 years, to another Deeside family who are in the position to do justice to it, he was still rightly discharging his responsibilities towards the people of Cromar, in whom he took such a deep interest.

Your old laird and friend has been able to go in and out amongst you to the very last. The call which so suddenly took him from his usual avocation here to the life of higher service beyond the veil, leaves no room for grief, but rather of profound thankfulness, and the wonderful tributes of affection and appreciation which have been paid to his memory and to the influence of his character and personality, not only by friends and neighbours, but by those he came into contact all over the world, will ever be a cherished heritage for those who loved him.

It is my high privilege as his life companion, to say to you all in his name and my own, 'Fare ye well-God be with you.'

I hope to reside amongst you for a few months more till the autumn, and you will know that till the end of the journey,

I am always your attached friend.

Ishbel Aberdeen and Temair

On 26 April, Rachel wrote to the editor of the Glasgow Bulletin to complain that an article written in response by a correspondent calling herself 'Northern Woman' had maligned her. She told her father that it had portrayed her as a grasping American hell-bent on chasing Lady Aberdeen out and seizing her domain.

In her letter to the Bulletin's readers Rachel said that she felt compelled to point out, as Lady Aberdeen had, that it was only due to Mac's generosity that Lord Aberdeen had been able to see out his days at Cromar. Their correspondent's remarks had also been misleading in other ways: although she was American, she had not spent any time in that country. She had been educated for the most part in Britain; she had attended Edinburgh University and had carried out much of her initial research in the Scottish Borders.

Lady Aberdeen had strength of character and great resilience, but she was under great stress. Not only did she face moving from her home, but she realized she would also have to leave behind the furniture, paintings and cherished possessions that she had failed to get exempted from the inventory all those years ago. Her only consolation came when Queen Mary paid her a visit on her last day at the House of Cromar and noticed a satinwood writing desk, a treasured gift from Lord Aberdeen. The Queen made Rachel an offer that she did not dare to refuse, and soon the secretaire, bought at market value, was on its way to Haddo. According to Marjorie Pentland, her mother confided in her diary that she had 'moments when one is near breaking down.'

Rachel was clearly sensitive to accusations that she had been ruthless in her dealings with a much-loved old lady, but it must be remembered that the MacRobert family and Trust had paid out a vast sum of money over the years on condition that they would one day own the estate.

The House of Cromar now became a base for her sons when they were in Aberdeenshire. Alasdair, his brothers and their friends only enjoyed its hospitality for a few years between 1934 when Ishbel left and 1941: by then all the boys were dead. That is why Rachel decided to put the house at the disposal of the RAF for use as a rest and recreation centre for men who had seen active service in the RAF and Allied Air Forces.

She had renamed it Alastrean, which in Latin means 'a place of honour by the hearth of the winged heroes of the stars'. Coincidently, or perhaps not, it also incorporates elements of the boys' names.

On 17 September 1941, she summoned Group Captain Finlay Crerar, CBE of the Air Ministry to see her and put her plan to him. She hoped her generous offer would show her support for her sons' comrades who 'magnificently continue the fight.' She said:

> In this house the boys had some happy gatherings of their friends and intended to have many more. They would undoubtedly have been gatherings of flying men. The fight must go on.

She explained why her choice of 'Alastrean' was appropriate in the circumstances, but added that she wished to keep the motto Mac had borrowed from the Clan Robertson, 'Virtutis Gloria Merces' – 'Glory is the Reward of Valour', solely for use at Alastrean.

The house opened on 15 June 1943 and could accommodate up to twenty guests at a time. It soon became a haven for traumatised servicemen, and two years later in November 1945, it welcomed its first Japanese prisoner of war who had been in captivity for four years. Of the many who followed, those who had been incarcerated in tropical countries seemed to benefit most from the bracing Aberdeenshire air. Guests of many different nationalities enjoyed their recuperation at Alastrean: among them were Australians, Norwegians, French, Polish and South Africans.

Although Alastrean House was a rest-home, the house rules were regimental. Guests were called at 8.00 a.m., the dressing gong sounded at 8.30 followed by the breakfast gong at 9.00 a.m. Water was rationed and guests were allowed only two baths per week. These had to be taken between 9 and 11 p.m. and water levels could not exceed 5–6 inches. However, their every other need was catered for.

While their mental and spiritual wellbeing was regarded as crucial to their recovery, their physical well-being was important too. To this end, each guest received a pint of milk daily during their stay and sport and recreation were seen as key factors in their recuperation.

Guests could only use the facilities in the recreation room between the hours of 2.30–4.00p.m. and 8.30–11.00 p.m but at other times there were many sports to be enjoyed. Tarland Golf Club made its nine-hole golf course available at no charge, while at Alastrean itself the men enjoyed chess, draughts, darts, miniature golf, and quoits. A pony and trap could be hired from the village. On the estate there was game shooting, fishing, croquet, walking and climbing, you would find plenty to occupy your time.

Rachel regularly visited and William Heughan provided the after-dinner entertainment. By 1948, officers and their wives were being offered holidays at Alastrean for a nominal fee, and by 1950 the women of the WRAF were allowed to stay too.

On 30 November 1952, forty-seven years to the day after Georgina died at Douneside, disaster struck: Alastrean House caught fire. The blaze started in the east wing and was discovered at 3 o'clock in the morning. As the telephone was not working, one of the staff had to drive into Tarland to raise the alarm at the police station. Ian and Alice Anderson watched the drama unfold from their cottage at Douneside where Norman, Alice's husband and Ian's father, was dairyman. Norman rushed to Alastrean with other men from the village to try to douse the flames before the local fire brigades arrived. It was just as well that the estate held regular fire drills and had its own fire fighting equipment, since the professional crews had to make hazardous journeys from Ballater and Aboyne on roads made treacherous by the freezing weather.

Vera Leslie, who still lives in Tarland, remembers waking up in her home close to Alastrean and seeing a pall of smoke hanging over the Howe. She and her family had heard nothing of the commotion in the middle of the night except for a loud bang which, they discovered later, was probably caused by a fire engine hitting a tree. Vera was given the sad news that one of her friends, had died in the blaze.

Margaret Baird, who was married to the handyman, had only started work there two weeks before. She tried to escape the flames by jumping from a window, but was found dead on the ground. Other staff members escaped with minor injuries: some had cut their wrists when they tried to break glass to get out of the building.

Alastrean House was gutted. A photograph in the *Dundee Courier* of 1 December 1952 shows only the porch and a few walls left standing. Alastrean cost £50,000 to rebuild and it did not reopen until 1958. Sadly, Rachel did not live to see the house restored.

CHAPTER 17

Looking After Her Ain

*I want you to have a better hall than any other village in Scotland and
I would like to see it an accomplished fact before I am too old to take
pleasure in your enjoyment.*

Rachel's philanthropy was not confined to RAF causes, but she was always
keen to ensure that there should be a connection with the family's
interests: a policy that is followed by the MacRobert Trust to this day.

Two ventures that fulfilled her criteria were the building of what became
the MacRobert Memorial Hall in Tarland and the MacRobert Hall at Robert
Gordon's College in Aberdeen. She took an active part in bringing each of
these projects to fruition, although neither was plain sailing and she encoun-
tered problems, misunderstandings and even hostility along the way.

This was particularly true in Tarland. Her generous gesture to the
community was made in good faith, but it led to considerable ill-feeling and
almost did not go ahead. However, the issues were not born of ingratitude,
but of misunderstandings.

Tarland boasted two halls: the village hall, known as the Cromar Hall,
and the Club Hall where the villagers could enjoy darts, whist, table tennis
and carpet bowls. During the Second World War, children from Aberdeen
who visited Tarland for a week's holiday enjoyed camping in the club house,
despite having to sleep on mattresses on the floor.

The Cromar Hall had been built in 1889 on ground probably donated
by Lord Aberdeen when the Court House which had stood on the site was
no longer needed. It was funded by money raised locally. Rachel proposed
a replacement. It would have more space but it had to incorporate the
original clock. In fact, after the work was finished, this was never the same
again, since the architect failed to allow enough room in his design to
accommodate the chimes and the sound they made was muffled.

This ambitious project began when William Heughan accompanied Rachel to see a play at the Cromar Hall. They enjoyed it, but the former actor remarked that it was a pity the community did not have a more suitable venue for such performances, especially one with a stage. Rachel immediately offered to fund a new hall and set about getting it built with her usual meticulous attention to detail.

Rachel's first step was to set up the Tarland Welfare Trust, making its board responsible for the property on the community's behalf. It would also administer the funds she gave although the provisions of the trust deed would absolve them of any financial liability that might arise. These conditions were accepted and agreed in a legally binding document which was signed in August 1951.

Over the course of the next few years, while building work was in progress, Mr Heughan made sure that the hall trustees adhered to Rachel's original wishes. She wanted the MacRobert family's own trustees to be represented on the board, along with a representative of the Union Bank of Scotland. She also laid down that, since the community was in charge, three local residents should be made trustees to ensure a fair balance of interests. She reserved the right to approve these appointments to herself and the other trustee. Funds would be provided when needed, but only with approval beforehand from her and the family trusts.

One of the Tarland Welfare Trust Committee's first decisions was to minute its determination to encourage women to become office bearers and to become involved in the running of the hall: a move that will undoubtedly have pleased its ex-Suffragette benefactor.

By September 1951, the permit to build had been granted and work steamed ahead. One milestone was the completion and formal opening of the Supper Room in July 1953. Rachel performed the formal opening ceremony but criticised the delays in her speech. The red tape involved had caused them and other frustrations, even though no Government grants had been requested or received. In the words quoted at the beginning of this chapter, she repeated her wish to present Tarland with 'a better hall than any other village in Scotland', yet she worried that her plan had been compromised by interfering bureaucrats.

There had also been some disagreements amongst the trustees. One objected to a plan to place an advertisement for a caretaker in national and local newspapers, saying that it was unconstitutional to go ahead with this until a public meeting had been held. He was overruled and the job was duly publicised in the *Scotsman*, the *Dundee Courier* and in the Aberdeen newspapers:

> Resident Caretaker for the MacRobert Memorial Hall, Tarland, all electric flat, heat and light provided; excellent opportunity for honest, sober and industrious man; would suit ex-policeman or ex-serviceman; age, experience etc. with three testimonials to the Chairman.

Before the interviews were held, the rules of the hall and the duties of its caretaker were agreed. Wages were to be two pounds per week with heat and light free of charge and two weeks' holidays. However, out of the thirty-eight applicants only two were considered and it took some time to find a suitable person to fulfil the post.

William Heughan, disconcerted by this and other small outbreaks of unrest, presumably spoke for Rachel when he warned: 'Any interference by troublemakers could have serious consequences.'

There was never any question of Rachel withholding her funds. Her initial donation of £6,000 made in April 1952 via the Sir Alexander MacRobert Memorial Trust was gratefully received:

> The Trustees of the Tarland Welfare Trust desire to express to Lady MacRobert and her fellow Trustees of the Sir Alexander MacRobert Memorial Trust their deepest gratitude for the magnificent gift of £6,000 as a first donation towards the cost of the MacRobert Memorial Hall and to assure Her Ladyship and her co—Trustees that they look on this wonderful gift as a sacred trust which they pledge themselves faithfully to administer in the interests of the MacRobert Memorial Hall which Her Ladyship has so much at heart.

The hall was eventually opened in April 1955, but Rachel, as she had feared, did not live to see it completed. The ceremony was performed by William Heughan, who said that he had been 'delighted and honoured' to accept the

Trustees invitation to become the hall's President. He struck a sourer note when he recalled the events that he claimed had almost scuppered Rachel's wish that the community should have 'a better hall than any other village in Scotland', but he then moved on to pay this tribute to Tarland's benefactor:

> I feel deeply moved. I feel it is impossible for me to take the place of the great hearted lady who is no longer with us. This Hall bears her name and that of her valiant sons. She knew the Tarland people better than they knew themselves. She did not look at your faults. She looked at your virtues. She wanted all of you to be happy.

The hall was well and truly christened when, on the day after its official opening, it reverberated to the sound of happy children having fun at a party. And in the evening the young of the community danced the night away.

The MacRobert patronage did not end there. The estate gave practical help with the painting and other maintenance work which helped to reduce costs. Even so, by 1958, four years after Rachel's death, the Sir Alexander MacRobert Memorial Trust and the MacRobert Trust between them had contributed more than £27,000 to the project: roughly £500,000 today. At Alasdair's coming of age party, Rachel had said that she wanted the amenities of Tarland and its surrounding area to be the benchmark against which those of other places might be judged. In building the hall, she had made sure that her ambition was handsomely fulfilled.

Earlier, she had had high hopes of a similar scheme: this time at Robert Gordon's College in Aberdeen.

'I trust that the fullest use will be made of it, so that the benefit to the students may be in proportion to the conception of those who were first inspired by a sense of its need,' she said.

In making a generous donation to the project, she was honouring one of Mac's wishes. Before he left Aberdeen for India, he had taught chemistry at evening classes at the college, but the clause in his will that provided for a legacy to the institution was ruled invalid under Indian law. So in 1925, when the college appealed for funds to build a new hall and other ancillary accommodation, she pledged £5,000.

Although there were also donations from the Former Pupils' Association and other benefactors, she later added a further £1,500. It brought her gift, allowing for interest accrued, to £7,200.

Rachel's plan was for the new hall to be used by the Secondary School and the Technical College. The project would include the building of a library, administrative offices and a board room and would be named the Rachel Workman MacRobert Hall in honour of their benefactor. The building would be erected on the west side of the College Avenue, partly on Blackfriars Street where Mac had lodged while teaching science at evening classes.

The foundation stone was laid by Mr W.W. McKechnie, Secretary of the Scottish Education Department. A casket was buried beneath it, containing a brochure prepared by the governors, copies of the prospectuses for 1929 and 1930 and a collection of newspapers and coins.

The ceremony, arranged to coincide with the college's bicentenary in December 1929 was attended by representatives from educational institutes as well as local magistrates, councillors and other dignitaries.

Mr McKechnie spoke in terms of which Mac would have approved. He exhorted the boys to remember that there was no room for the slacker. The happy man was the busy man. School and college were opportunities. They must not blame others and should not 'grouse'. He saw physical fitness as beneficial to study and encouraged them to work hard, and to do so not only for their own sakes but for those of their school, their city and their country.

The hall was designed by Robert Leslie Rollo, Head of the School of Architecture and a governor of Robert Gordon's. Three doors led to a large vestibule and on into the hall, cloakrooms and a library. A separate door allowed access to the stage and dressing rooms so that productions of plays could be mounted. There was room for art exhibitions and much thought had been given to acoustics and lighting. The hall could seat 800 people, with an additional 200 in the gallery: it could accommodate the whole school for assemblies and serve as a room in which examinations, concerts, and rehearsals for choirs and orchestras could be held.

The building was sympathetically designed to complement the existing school buildings on the campus in Schoolhill. Rachel approved, praising it as a 'worthy addition which will be a lasting exposition of the skill of your architect, Mr Rollo.'

In March 1931, it was complete. The official opening was conducted by Rachel who was accompanied by the young Sir Alasdair. The Chairman of the Governors Mr Walter A. Reid thanked her not only for her financial generosity, but also for the interest she had taken in the project. He described her as 'gracious, and dignified' and added that she had carried out the negotiations over her donations with a 'complete absence of ostentation'. Rachel in reply described the college's progress over the last 200 years and she also took the opportunity to make a plea for more funds so that further capital development could take place.

Rachel also gave to more modest causes. In 1949, a young man called Henry Gray from Craigievar was competing in the games events at the Tarland show when, to his consternation, a message came over the tannoy asking him to report to the secretary's tent. He was new on the Highland Games circuit and assumed he had done something wrong. He answered the summons with some trepidation.

He was met by William Heughan who told him that Rachel had been impressed by his performance in the ring and wished to speak to him. She told him that she was a Patron of the Aboyne Games and was keen for him to compete there. When Henry confessed he had no kilt to wear, he was told to visit Mr Blackhall, the Tarland tailor where a kilt was duly made for him in the Robertson tartan at Her Ladyship's expense. A grateful Henry remembers her as very approachable and natural when he went to Douneside to convey his thanks to her personally.

Although Henry failed to do well at Aboyne – he felt uncomfortable wearing the kilt for the first time and stood in awe of the mighty stalwarts against whom he was competing – he was soon winning prizes with the rest of them. In 1953 he broke the heavy hammer record at the Aboyne Games and reached the pinnacle of success the following year when he became the Scottish Heavy Events Champion, his proudest achievement. Today he is a respected judge on the Highland Games circuit and a living legend.

CHAPTER 18

A Job Well Done

*A good business woman interested in large scale farming and stock
raising and in food production.*

When the National Society of New England Women awarded Rachel
their medal of honour after she donated the Stirling Bomber to the
RAF, they also paid tribute to another of her achievements. The young
woman who had been reluctant to become involved in the ownership and
management of her husband's estate had become a force to be reckoned
with in agriculture, not only in Scotland but much further afield.

When Alasdair came of age in 1933, John McArthur, speaking on behalf
of the tenants of the Douneside and Melgum estates, praised her efforts.
She was, he said, a perfectionist, which meant that operations were labour
intensive if her high standards were to be met. This meant plenty of jobs:
a godsend to Cromar in difficult times. Thanks to the acquisition of
Melgum, there were now over 1,000 acres under the plough. By 1950, after
yet more land had been purchased, the estate, operating under the umbrella
of the parent group, The MacRobert Trust, was farming around 2,200 acres.
Forty-three farms, crofts and grazings were let to 'suitable tenants', while a
manager looked after the interests of the Home Farm at Douneside and a
further twelve in-hand farms.

Rachel's approach was imaginative and pragmatic. During the Second
World War she gave over the lawn at Douneside to growing potatoes and
had a dairy built on the tennis court. Undoubtedly her most important
innovation was the Alamein Agricultural Training Group. She had particularly
relished the allied victory at El Alamein in 1942, not least because 'her'
Hurricanes had been deployed at this turning point in the North Africa
campaign. The venture, founded in 1944, was based at Easter Knowehead,
and by 1951 five farms were involved in providing free training for young
men who were interested in pursuing a career in farming.

The Alamein training course soon attracted attention. In April 1946, in a debate in the House of Commons about the problems of attracting new workers to agriculture, Colin Thornton Kemsley, MP for Aberdeenshire and Kincardine West, contrasted the failure of the government's Agricultural Training Scheme with Rachel's successful initiative on the Douneside estate. Twenty-four ex-servicemen had been recruited but, he complained, the ministries in distant Whitehall were proving reluctant to help her:

'She wanted to call it the El Alamein Training Centre, and she approached the Ministry of Labour. She said, "I will build accommodation for these men, provided I can have some huts as a temporary measure. I will provide the instruction. The farms are here, the herds are here, and we will give them the finest training in the land." What happened? She went to the Ministry of Labour last summer but was unable to get any satisfactory response from them, so she went to the Department of Agriculture, who said: "It will be a good idea. Let us have a conference on the site. We will get all the interested parties. We will get the agricultural executive committees, the Ministry of Labour representative and everybody who is concerned in any way. They can all come down and we can talk it over on the premises." Nothing further happened. In September, Lady MacRobert wanted to know what was being done, so she asked the Department. They said: "We think we had better postpone the conference. We are not getting many applicants." Another letter came the following month. Letters came at monthly intervals, all saying: "Sorry but we think we had better postpone the matter, as we are not getting enough applicants." I took the matter up. The Joint Under-Secretary of State for Scotland very kindly promised me that someone would go down and have a talk with Lady MacRobert. Very nearly three quarters of a year have passed, but absolutely nothing has been done.

'I cannot help thinking that if any imagination had been shown about this matter, all the interested parties would have gone there and shown that they appreciated the generous offer that had been made. They would have thrashed out the proposal, worked out some scheme, and advertised it locally. I am sure that local people, and especially men of the 51st Highland Division, would have been keen to go to a centre called the El Alamein Training Centre to learn about farming. Nothing has happened. It is typical of the lack of imagination and of determination which the Government are showing in connection with the training scheme.'

Rachel carried on regardless. When the students had completed their studies, they tackled the practical side of their course on the estate. They came from very different backgrounds and boarded at various farms in the district, including Ranna and Culsh. Alice Anderson, whose husband Norman looked after Rachel's Freisian dairy herd at Kincraigie recalls that during the turnover time in the summer when some students departed and others replaced them, she could have about sixteen lads to feed, although usually there were eight.

Although one young man thought farming a filthy, dirty job, most were good-hearted young lads. One, who came from Shetland, arranged for a barrel of salt herring to be taken down on the boat. It was duly picked up at Aberdeen Harbour by Norman and Alice and while this helped the generous donor to overcome homesickness, the saltiness of the fish did not go down well in the Howe of Cromar. Others found settling in much harder: one suddenly up-tailed and was off to catch the bus home.

A rather more notable ex-serviceman recruited by Rachel was Flight Lieutenant Bill Reid, VC who originally came to Alastrean House to recuperate after his wartime experiences. He had won the Victoria Cross for his bravery in a famous raid on Dusseldorf involving 600 bombers. The citation reads:

> Wounded in two attacks, without oxygen suffering severely from the cold, his navigator dead, his wireless operator fatally wounded, his aircraft crippled and defenceless, Flight Lieutenant Reid showed superb courage and leadership in penetrating a further 200 miles into enemy territory to attack one of the most strongly defended targets in Germany, every additional mile increasing the hazard of the long and perilous journey home. This tenacity and devotion to duty were beyond praise.

Bill Reid spent time at Alastrean recovering from his injuries, and in December 1943, in recognition of this supreme act of bravery and exemplary leadership by a Scottish youth, Rachel and the Trustees chose him to be the first recipient of the MacRobert's Reply Award. On his return to duty he was posted to the famous '617 Dambuster' squadron. He served with it until the following July when he crash-landed in Germany. He was taken prisoner and incarcerated in Stalag Luft 111. Freedom came when the camp near Berlin to which he had been transferred was liberated by the Russians. After the war, Reid studied at Glasgow University and at the West of Scotland Agricultural College and won a scholarship from the Lady MacRobert Special Trust Fund to travel to India, North America and New Zealand to study farming methods. In 1950, he became the manager of Douneside and Ranna Farms and subsequently became a Director of the MacRobert Farm Company.

Rachel also encouraged success in smaller-scale ventures in Tarland. She donated trophies to the village's annual horticultural and agricultural shows that are keenly contested to this day. Her interest in agriculture and gardening was not superficial. She ran the estate as a business and her standards were exacting. Once, she dispensed with the services of a solicitor who was unable to answer a question she posed on an unannounced visit. She took exception to his need to bring in one of his staff to deal with her query. She rewarded diligent workers by leaving them to their own devices.

Norman Leslie was Rachel's farm secretary and he was often summoned to the house to go over the books with her. Her Ladyship meant what she said, he remembers: if she said 'no', she meant 'no'; and if she said 'yes', you went and got on with it. Rachel's father was well aware of this side of his daughter's character. He once wrote,

'She has developed all the decision of character of her mother with a great deal of scientific knowledge to back it … She is thoroughly decided and knows quite as much as Fanny did, and is more forward in pushing for it.'

Vera Leslie's father was gamekeeper to 'Lady Mac', as she was known locally. She recollects how impressed he was by Rachel's knowledge and willingness to learn.

Determined and focused as she was, Rachel had a soft side too. She kept a legion of cats at Douneside. To say they were well looked after is putting it mildly. From one innocuous stray upon which the dairyman took pity, there grew a huge colony. People in Tarland still remember how they lived the life of Riley. At one time, two crates of milk were brought down from the big dairy for them every day and the gamekeeper was instructed to

166

deliver dead rabbits for their consumption. Rachel loved the cats so much that her favourite, Carrie, is buried close to her at Douneside. The creatures also had William Heughan wrapped round their paws and he encouraged them to take up residence in the house.

The estate was a hive of activity. Hugh Brown from Tarland worked at Douneside as a youth, apprenticed to his father who was the painter on the estate. Like Norman, he remembers that Rachel was a formidable woman, although she was fair. While she did much to ensure that the residents of Tarland were gainfully employed, if an employee's face did not fit, they did not last long at Douneside.

The success of the pedigree herds meant a host of extra small jobs for the estate staff: among them, making name boards for the shows and a box to hold the Aberdeen Angus cup presented to the Royal Northern Agricultural Society in Aberdeen. The joiners were always busy. They made dog kennels for the keeper, new chicken houses and broody cages for the poultry farm, glass was cut for the incubators and the pigs were provided with a new straw haik, a rack or manger for holding fodder.

Other workers laid sewage systems and repaired the estate roads. Ian Anderson of Kincraigie recalled that the condition of the properties and lands on the estate was at least as good as any in the neighbourhood, if not better.

The estate mechanics were kept particularly busy. Hugh Brown remembers how 'Lady Mac' would drive herself in her little red Fiat, but the estate also had a blue Fiat 1500, a red Fiat 500, a Triumph 1800, Austin 10 saloons and Ford and Humber Super Snipe shooting brakes, as well as two motorcycles, one of which was used by the gamekeeper. The Leyland 5-ton lorry and the Austin lorry, the Fordson van and the Reliant 5 cwt van were all in regular use and needed to be serviced and repaired. In April 1952 there were three tractors at Ranna, four at Easttown, two at West Davoch and one each at Old Mill, Melgum and Boig and two for the use of the estate in general. The mechanics also had to tend the power plant, the lighting plant, the milking machines and the lawn mowers.

After the great gale of January 1953 which devastated the woods of North East Scotland, the foresters cleared 396,700 cubic feet of timber in less than a year.

The gardeners were busy too as Rachel transformed the surroundings of Douneside House. In 1914, the 'diary' written on behalf of two-year old Alasdair noted that 'there is an awful lot of trees planted below the rock garden which is newly fenced and wired. Pratt and Urquhart are digging, levelling and pulling out loose stones.

Rachel described how she set about the task in a talk to the Tarland WRI in September 1949:

> When I first came to live here, there were no trees except three at the front of the house. The Terrace had the same circular seat it still has and was entirely of grass. There was an unbroken view of the hills in the direction of the Drive and the Gatehouse Lodge. Sir Alexander was very fond of rare trees, and soon we decided to lay out a landscape garden; bit by bit, rare trees from all parts were added – many of which had only been brought into this country a few years before. Many of the shrubs did not survive and it became a case of survival of the fittest. You have seen how these matured and grew into a perfect blend of shape and colour, and acted as shelter to Douneside. Whichever way the winds may blow, it is always possible to find a sheltered corner to sit and rest and meditate. When one first plants trees and lays out pleasure grounds, it is necessary to try and visualise what such plantations will look like and grow into – say 20, 30 or 40 years afterwards. It is only then that one can judge whether the original plan has taken shape as intended and a successful result obtained.

In fact, Georgina had begun the work, but after her first visit to Douneside, Rachel had set out to learn more about alpine and glacial botany. Later, her friends the Cudworths, who had a beautiful garden in York, provided her with cuttings to grow on and plant at Douneside. But there were structural problems to solve:

> I decided that the gully next the house where the stream ran down to join the Tarland Burn, must be put to better use than as a receptacle for farm rubbish of every sort thrown into it. So a new venture was started, and the Rock Garden of which there were only two in Scotland at that time came into being.

Our little glen became transformed with miniature rock cliffs, waterfalls, two lakes, bridges and rocky eminences planted with rare miniature trees and plants of every sort. Each year I collected more and more on my travels, until there were over 1,000 different varieties of rock plants. This garden I tended entirely myself for many years, until things grew up and became well established. Between 1934 and 1940 Mr Heughan assisted me with his valuable advice on landscape gardening, and many alterations and innovations were made in the layout. It was then that the old original walled farm garden was made into the terraced Rose Garden which has become one of the features of Douneside ... It is my wish and hope that Douneside and the Gardens will be preserved; the trees, the lawns, the flowers and the house will all have their story for those who can understand.

In 1992, an extra adornment was added to Rachel's horticultural legacy. Candy Richardson, wife of Sir Robert who was the Administrator at the Trust at that time, thought it would be fitting to mark the MacRobert Trust's Golden Jubilee by having a rose named in Rachel's honour. Together they approached Cocker's Roses, the famous rose growers from Aberdeen, who agreed to provide the rose and donate two pounds to the Trust from every rose sold. After the short list had been whittled down to three, Lady Wakeford, the wife of the Chairman of the Trust, chose a floribunda which, according to the catalogue description, had 'blooms of light apricot colouring' and 'light green semi glossy' foliage. In the middle of a ferocious hailstorm, the roses were planted in new beds on the lawn in front of Douneside House. Bert Paterson had newly retired from his position as Head Gardener and was honoured to be asked back to plant one of the new roses.

Rachel made sure that life was not all work and no play for her employees. Lord and Lady Aberdeen had provided the community with many facilities and Rachel ensured that they continued to benefit from the estate. Groups such as the dramatic society and the choral society could meet in the Hall and there were opportunities for more active pursuits. In 1927, the King spearheaded a campaign to encourage sport and recreation in rural districts. The Club building which Lord Aberdeen had provided was soon outgrown. Rachel responded to the appeal by donating more ground and a new hall and pavilion were erected and tennis courts laid out.

In May 1946, Tarland Football Club was given tenure of the football pitch but, because there was much controversy over the playing of football on a Sunday, Rachel and the Trustees adopted the same stance as the Football Association and the SFA in prohibiting football to be played on the Sabbath.

That same year, when the County Council wanted to build a school kitchen and dining hall, the land was duly provided and a similar deal was done so that council houses could be erected. This landlord with a social conscience also liked to see the community having fun. At Christmas, there was a party for the children hosted by Her Ladyship, and every December the men of the estate staff were invited to take part in a hare hunt.

But there was one enterprise that Rachel enjoyed most of all: she became a cattle breeder. The Douneside herds are an important part of her legacy.

CHAPTER 19

The Herds – Her Other Legacy

Lady MacRobert is so enthusiastic and so well known to and respected by British agriculturalists that the council recommends her election as president with all confidence.

The herd of pedigree British Friesian cattle that Rachel bought to provide milk for the ailing baby Alasdair in 1913 was housed at Douneside. Right from the start she took a personal interest in the animals and derived great pleasure from grooming them. She even wrote to Mac in India to describe in great detail what pedigree Friesian Herd registration documents looked like.

Over the years, thanks to a judicious breeding programme and a well-thought-out feeding regime, the yield and quality of milk from the herd improved dramatically. In 1931, Rachel was very proud when six of her Douneside heifers achieved a United Kingdom record by each producing 1,500 gallons of milk. Four years later, the average amount of milk from the whole herd was 1,122 gallons.

She enjoyed giving visitors to Douneside tours of her farming enterprise, but the welfare of the herd was her main priority. The Douneside team became leaders in animal husbandry, and their ideas, such as the establishment of a nursery for the calves, were innovative and ahead of their time. For example, when they saw that the stock bull was uncomfortable on the cobbled floor of his pen and was therefore in danger of injuring his legs, they had the cobbles replaced with concrete flooring. And everything possible, of course, was done to facilitate the mating process: a service pen was constructed in a corner in the hope that it would 'help this business considerably'.

Rachel invested heavily to ensure that the herd maintained its attested status. Because stringent measures had to be observed, double fencing was erected in 1949 to prevent contact with any neighbouring cattle. She made sure that top quality animals with the best breeding potential were sought out and purchased, and her experience as a scientist stood her in good stead in the selecting of bloodlines for the herd's foundation stock.

But the real experts at Douneside were her cattlemen. One of them was Norman Anderson, who came to work with the Friesians at Douneside in 1947. Norman and his wife Alice lived at the Mains of Kincraigie, where the herd was later located. They found that getting the milk to Aberdeen was no simple matter. The churns were filled in the dairy and loaded onto a horse-drawn cart. This took them to the road to meet Shand's bus, which then took them to Aboyne station for the train journey to the Twin Spires creamery in Aberdeen. Their son Ian, who went on to play an important part in the life of the herd, recalls how, after heavy snowfalls, he had to pick up the empty churns from wherever they had been dropped off and haul them back across the fields to the farm. In 1985, when the Trust ceased its direct farming operations and the herd was dispersed, Ian took over the dairy at Mains of Kincraigie thus maintaining the tradition of dairy farming in the Anderson name.

But there was more to the herd's success than breaking records for the quality and quantity of the milk it produced. The Douneside strain of Friesian cattle became renowned throughout the world. On 3 November 1937 at the York show and sale, Douneside Lodbert, an eleven-month-old bull which came from a long line of top-class milk yielding dairy cows, was reserve male champion and sold for 130 guineas to Douneside. He was virtually unbeatable in the show ring and made a great difference to the breeding programme. In fact, he was so valued by Rachel that when he died in 1946 she decided to preserve his memory in a rather unusual way. She told her trustees at their annual general meeting in December 1947:

> Douneside Lodbert – this famous show and stock bull which died of old age in May 1946 has in a sense returned to us. His wonderful head has been preserved and mounted and at present hangs in the farm office.

The herd travelled the country, and over a three-year spell in which they competed at the Royal Highland, the Great Yorkshire and the English Royal

Shows, the Friesians won a total of fifty-three first prizes, fourteen cups, six championships and eighteen medals including a gold, as well as £800 in prize money.

Even farmer Rob Dinnie from Birse, whose ancestor Donald Dinnie famously lifted the Dinnie stones remembers being rather in awe of the men who led these ponderous animals round the show ring, especially the bulls whose massive power was rather intimidating to the onlooker.

Rachel was devoted to the breed and her support and encouragement of her stockmen was unstinting.

She donated a trophy to the Royal Highland Show to be awarded to the Supreme Champion chosen from the British Friesian classes. She researched the patterns of ancient Scottish cowbells at the National Museum of Antiquities of Scotland in Edinburgh and then commissioned a silversmith to design and make a cup embellished with embossed, interlaced Celtic designs. She named it the MacRobert Champion Silver Bell.

In 1937, in the words quoted at the beginning of this chapter, the Council of the British Friesian Cattle Society recommended to their fellow-members that they should elect Rachel as their President. This was an acknowledgement not only of her expertise in cattle breeding, but also of the esteem in which she was held by the agricultural community. She duly assumed office at the Annual General Meeting in February 1937 and served for two years.

Rachel's interest was not confined to one breed, however. Like the Friesians, her herd or fold of Highland Cattle at Douneside became internationally famous. She founded it to help preserve the breed by preventing many of the old family lines from dying out. She knew that the best way to achieve this would be to improve the quality of the animals without compromising their character or hardiness.

She did wonder if the land at Douneside would suit them, but after researching the history of the breed, she devised a system which she called 'Lines and Links' to help her to identify and buy suitable breeding lines.

Rachel began to form this herd in 1950, when animals from the lines she wished to use as her foundation stock came up for sale. She knew that the quality of the stock bull would be critical to success, and in 1951 at the

Oban sales she found it: She purchased Victor of Gylen, whose placing in the show ring and the price he made at the sale that followed, were not without controversy. He cost Rachel 550 guineas.

Three years later, the judge's son, John McKechnie, came to Douneside to manage the Highland fold. While he waited to take up the position, Fred Paterson of Easttown, who looked after Douneside's herd of 120 commercial cows and their followers, was asked to bring out the bull in his first show season at Douneside. The estate, Fred and his wife Helen remember, looked after its employees well. Milk, firewood and tatties were the perks of the job and they were allowed to keep twelve hens and pullets – although no one ever checked to see if this number had been exceeded. In exchange, workers were expected to observe Rachel's request that there be no mechanical noise to disturb the peace on a Sunday and between 1 and 2 p.m. daily while she was taking a rest.

He recalls, as do others, that to those who pulled their weight she was a fair boss, much interested in the work of her farms.

Victor's first outing was to the Highland Show which was held in Aberdeen that year and which will always be remembered for the rain. While Fred describes how easily Victor saw off his rivals, his wife Helen remembers it for the amount of washing of muddy clothes she had to do. Victor and Fred then went on to the Royal Show, which was held that year in Cambridge. The great bull was loaded onto the train at Aboyne, but his success there made the journey worthwhile. When he died, Victor's head, like Lodbert's, was stuffed and hung on the wall at the estate office at Balmuir.

John McKechnie's arrival at Douneside ensured that the fold became recognised throughout the world. He came from a family of renowned breeders and his immense knowledge won him the Ormsary prize for his outstanding contribution to the commercial wellbeing of Highland cattle.

In 1962 the estate entered the export market after Baron C. Rosenorn-Lehn got in touch to enquire about buying Highland heifers and a stock bull for his estate in Denmark. McKechnie chose five heifers and, after many to-ings and fro-ings, they were duly despatched.

As a boy, William Heughan was fascinated by cattle and he went on in later years to take a particular interest in the Galloway breed. He accompanied Rachel to her first Oban bull sale and he remained an enthusiastic supporter of the Highland Cattle breed even after her death. In 1966, the Lady MacRobert Special Trust paid 900 guineas for the outstanding show bull, Exhibit of Strathallan. He went on to sire five consecutive bull sale champions, thanks to John McKechnie's expert husbandry.

In the sale ring, Douneside bulls broke records. In 1973, Glen Osprey Farm from Ontario, Canada, paid 2,400 guineass for Leodhas of Douneside. The following year, a bull from Douneside stock did even better by fetching 2,800 guineas.

In 1986, the Trust changed its farming policy and let some units on a limited partnership basis. John McKechnie took on West Knowehead and bought the twenty-five cows from the fold, ensuring the survival of the Douneside line. When John McKechnie died unexpectedly in 1991, his neighbours the Allardyces of East Town, who were already in partnership with the Trust, continued the tradition of Highlanders in the Howe by purchasing twelve of them from West Knowehead. The MacRobert Perpetual Challenge Bowl, presented by the MacRobert Trust in memory of Rachel, is still awarded in the Highland Cattle section at the Royal Highland Show. It goes to the best group bred by one exhibitor.

With Friesians at Douneside and Highlanders at Knowehead, Rachel's third pure-bred herd, of Aberdeen Angus cattle, was kept at West Davoch. It was established with about a dozen cows in 1932 when the neighbouring Melgum Estate was sold. The herd expanded rapidly with purchases from other notable breeders and in 1938 it boasted some sixty cows. Once again, Rachel researched the blood lines for her foundation stock and soon animals from the herd began to make their mark at shows and sales. Their dominance of the show circuit and supremacy at the sales was due not only to Rachel's willingness to pay for the best cattle, but also to the work of first class stockmen such as Gavin Ogg, Geordie Cowe, William Shand, and in later years, Henry Durward, who during a lifetime of devotion to the breed, won the coveted Herdsman's Challenge Cup at Perth.

William Heughan helped too. He had his own, albeit not exactly innovative, method of choosing pedigree bulls. He looked at their pedigrees. He also chose their names. Although he only visited the herd twice a year, before the Highland Show and the Perth Bull sales, the stockmen acknowledged and respected his expertise.

There were many males and females from the herd which would long be remembered as outstanding animals. Their dominance of the show circuit and supremacy at the sales was due to the farming enterprise having the wherewithal to fund the purchase of quality stock such as Emor of Derculich, purchased in 1948 at the Perth bull sales for the vast sum of 7,100 guineas. He had stood reserve champion and his progeny, both male and female, made a significant impact on Aberdeen Angus breeding lines.

The benefits of breeding pedigree stock of this quality had a similar effect on the commercial herd. Bulls were normally used on the pedigree cows for about three years when they would then join the commercial herd and produce quality cross cattle.

The season of 1950 was marked by so many successes for the Aberdeen Angus that the Cromar, Upper Dee and Donside Agricultural Association held a 'complimentary banquet for Lady MacRobert and William Heughan' in the village hall in Tarland on 2 August that year. The evening began when Mr Peter McFarlane, the estate factor and chairman for the evening, called on Flight Lieutenant Bill Reid, VC, the manager of Douneside and Ranna farms, to regale those gathered with the details of the success of the herd at Turriff Show the previous day. Of the seven animals entered, six had been first in their class and the seventh had been second.

Then Councillor Alexander J Blackhall, from Millhead, Tarland, offered the congratulations of the community. He said:

> The herd at Douneside, as it were, is only a youngster, being young in comparison to many of the great herds of Aberdeen Angus cattle scattered throughout the length and breadth of this country, and it is all the more reason why we should be proud of the fact that during the shows of this year, they not only have swept the boards at the local shows at home, but they have gone abroad, away down to the Highland and the Royal English Shows where they have swept everything before them.

In another speech, Duncan Reid, on behalf of the tenants, described

Rachel as 'a sport', adding, 'She takes her wins with modesty and her defeats, if any, with a smile.'

When she spoke, Rachel thanked her team of stockmen and said that her ambition had been to 'establish a herd of Aberdeen Angus cattle of such quality and breeding that owners and breeders from all over the world would wish to come to the original district when they required to replenish their herds with true native Aberdeen blood.'

Yet two years earlier, the herd had been reduced as it had outgrown its accommodation. Forty-two females were sold at Aberdeen ensuring that the Douneside bloodlines were dispersed throughout the country.

The herd continued to win prizes after Rachel's death and the bloodlines she developed are still important to the breed today. Although the herd won almost every prestigious trophy available to Aberdeen Angus cattle, the most coveted of them all, the Supreme Championship at the Perth Bull Sales eluded the MacRobert Farms until 1964. The winner, Essidium of Douneside was purchased by Black Watch Farms of New York for the sum of 54,000 guineas. At the time, this was the third highest price ever paid for a bull: the first and second were all held by the Aberdeen Angus breed.

Top price was one of the few accolades that eluded Rachel in her forty years of success during her life, but it is testimony to the skill and foresight that made her one of Scotland's most noteworthy cattle breeders.

CHAPTER 20

An End and A Beginning

A mother whose life was full of sacrifice and tragedy but who by God's help turned weeping into defiance and defeat into victory.

Rachel's father confided in his sister, albeit grudgingly, that his assessment of his daughter in her youth had been wrong.

'She may not have been a very bright student,' he wrote. 'She showed no ability indeed was rather stupid, but since she has matured she has evidently done work that has distinguished her and she has become acquainted with many leading scientists.'

Perhaps Rachel was indeed a late-developer, but she made her mark on Britain both during and after World War II.

On the evening of the 31 August 1954, her Aberdeen Angus bull, Remormon of Douneside, was filmed as the breed's representative at the London Smithfield Cattle Show held at Earls Court. His appearance on TV screens was a notable event in the pioneering days of television and a coup for the herd. But the next day, Rachel died suddenly at Douneside of a heart attack. She was seventy.

'Div ye nae ken the Lady's deid?' was the admonishment to a group of small boys capering on their way home from Tarland school on the day her funeral took place at Douneside. The service was conducted by the Reverend Ricketts, the minister of Craigiebuckler Church in Aberdeen. With him was the Reverend J. Duncan of the Kalimpong Homes in India, which Rachel had continued to support since Mac's death. The funeral was a celebration of the life of the 'fairy godmother of the RAF' and many dignitaries attended from the organisations that she had also favoured with her patronage.

Rachel had been a benefactor of the Ballater branch of the Air Training Corps Pipe Band, which was now called upon to play. As the haunting notes of the Skye Boat Song, her favourite tune, drifted across the valley in mournful lament for her passing, those who loved, admired, and respected her gathered round her grave to say their final farewells. To another lament, The Flowers of the Forest, a piece of MacRobert tartan was laid on her coffin, which was made from Deeside oak. Nine Meteor jets from RAF Leuchars flew low overhead in a poignant and fitting gesture to the lady whose remains were now laid to rest in the tranquillity of the grounds at Douneside, overlooking the lands she had come to love.

In paying tribute to Rachel who had done so much to support its cause, a representative from Robert Gordon's College said, 'Her personal charm, great business ability and generosity contributed largely to the welfare of the community.' The words quoted at the top of the chapter, spoken by the Reverend Ricketts, recognised her achievements in several different spheres.

Rachel was brought up by a mother with a strong interest in feminist causes, and as a young woman, she was actively involved in the Suffragette movement in York. She was President of the Women's United Front, an organisation that fought for women's rights and she became the President of the International Women's Day National Committee in 1943, the year it published her book Women on the March.

She was used to asserting her beliefs, so it is perhaps not surprising that she became one of the first women to hold office in several previously male-dominated organisations that recognised her ability and sought her support. When Rachel married Mac she knew nothing of farming, managing the land, or indeed livestock breeding, but she became respected and successful in all three. The British Friesian Cattle Society recognised her worth as did the Royal Northern Agricultural Society which, in December 1937, appointed her as its first woman President. And if proof were needed of her ability to meet the challenges of the job, it came when she was subsequently elected for a second term of office. The Scottish Chamber of Agriculture was also pleased to invite her into the fold: she was one of the first three women they honoured in this way.

She never forgot her training as a research scientist and she put the skills she learned to good use when developing the 'lines and links' system for her cattle-breeding programme. Her pedigree herds were more than a business enterprise to her: she genuinely loved her animals, and she supported her cattlemen at shows and sales throughout the land with boundless enthusiasm.

She inspired others. Her support of the war effort in the air was not only financial: she travelled the country giving of her time to rally support for the armed forces and urging continuing defiance of Hitler and the Nazis. She was appointed as the first President of the Aberdeen branch of the Royal Air Force Association and was seen as an obvious choice for the presidency of the Spitfire-Mitchell memorial fund, set up to commemorate the life of Reginald Mitchell who designed the famous fighter aircraft, recognised as the backbone of Fighter Command. This, and her famously generous gift of a Stirling bomber, and later four Hawker Hurricanes, led to an invitation to become the first female President of the British Aeromodellers Association, a role which she readily accepted.

Mac was not the only member of the family who was held in high regard by Aberdeen University. In October 1942 when Lord Louis Mountbatten, who was then serving his country as Chief of Combined Operations withdrew his candidature for the Rectorship, Rachel was nominated for the post by the students in recognition of the interest she took in their welfare and of her campaign to boost morale during the war. Her bid was unsuccessful: Sir Richard Stafford Cripps topped the vote. He had been despatched to Moscow as British Ambassador in 1940, and such were his diplomatic skills that when the Nazis invaded, an alliance was quickly formed between the western allies and the Soviet Union.

Although her commitment to the war effort made her a public figure, Rachel was constant in her support of the local area. In 1936, her neighbour Lord Aberdeen, Lord Lieutenant of Aberdeenshire, recommended that she be appointed as a Justice of the Peace, and she also served as Honorary President of the Cromar Nursing Association. The war memorial where the names of Roderic and Iain record that they laid down their lives for their country, stands sentinel outside the Village Hall. It bears the family name, which will always be remembered in Tarland.

Perhaps the most significant of all the honours accorded to her and to the Trust she created came long after Rachel's death, when, in September 1998, The Queen and Prince Philip broke into their summer holiday at Balmoral to make a special visit to Tarland. After planting a tree in the garden at Alastrean House, they stood on the lawn at Douneside as the latest MacRobert's Reply, a Tornado GR1 aircraft based at RAF Lossiemouth, swooped above them in a poignant salute to the family that had lost yet given so much.

Rachel's foresight and ability to think to the future are what make her one of the most outstanding women of her time. Her background was very different to that of the typical Scottish landowner or business tycoon. Because she was an outsider she could cast a fresh eye upon the problems faced by the people around her. She was not afraid of lateral thinking, nor of ruffling feathers if necessary in a good cause. Her robust, direct and innovative approach to philanthropy is still admired today, not least by those who run Britain's other charities: many have taken inspiration from her for their own work. Perhaps it is best summed up in a phrase that she hoped would guide her trustees as they made their dispensations: 'new situations create new challenges'. In this spirit, the various Trusts she set up have provided funds to initiate and support cultural, social, agricultural and military causes both great and small.

Rachel was following in Mac's footsteps, but hers was an even more vigorous and imaginative philanthropy. It helped of course that she had a far greater sum of money to work with. She was a very rich woman in her own right having inherited a fortune from her father. As well as her properties in the United Kingdom, she had accumulated estate in Canada, the USA, South Africa, Australia and Jersey.

Not only did she set about putting her combined inheritances to good use in her lifetime but in 1943 she began to put her affairs in order: a move that ensured her assets could be appropriately assigned on her death. Her first step was to establish the MacRobert Trust which was designed to help members of the armed forces and those of the Mercantile Marine and Women's Services. It would also provide grants to a wide range of charitable organisations, particularly those associated with the armed forces, education, hospitals and agriculture. The fund also paid for the running costs of Alastrean House, which had been turned into a recreation centre and holiday home for RAF and Commonwealth air crew. When she died, £100,000 of her £633,950 fortune was bequeathed to this Trust.

The Sir Alexander MacRobert Memorial Trust was founded at the same time, and the shares it held in his British India Corporation represented a controlling interest in the company. It is not surprising therefore, that it was required to pay half its income into the other MacRobert Trusts. On Rachel's death, it received seven parts of ten of the residue of her estate; the other three were given as personal bequests.

To ensure the future of the family home, Rachel formed the Douneside Trust, and stipulated that the investments that she gave it should be divided into two funds: one to maintain the house and its outbuildings and the other to help cadet and youth organisations.

On 26 July 1943, she wrote to all her workers on the Douneside group of farms explaining that the farming operations would now be carried out under MacRobert Farms (Douneside) Ltd and in an emotional statement said:

> You are engaged in highly vital work. By your work you can help me to 'Reply' in yet another way to the terrible enemy who would like to destroy you and all of us if he could. Our food production will help to bring nearer the day of victory.

Perhaps it was no coincidence that the Lady MacRobert Special Trust was set up in 1950, the year of her herd's greatest successes in the show ring. This was expected to assist the MacRobert and Douneside Trusts and in addition, was to focus its support on rural and land-based industries, including – to the surprise of no one – pedigree stock-breeding.

At a dinner held in August 1950 to recognise the outstanding achievements of her pedigree herds, the chairman for the evening, Peter McFarlane, factor for the MacRobert estate, announced to those gathered in the MacRobert Hall in Tarland that a highly unusual and significant honour had been bestowed upon Rachel.

"On the death of Sir Alexander, Baronet of Cawnpore and Cromar, the Baronetcy passed in turn to his three sons, Sir Alasdair, Sir Roderic and Sir Iain who, as last Baronet, was killed in action over the North Sea; no living person was entitled to use the Baronet's Arms, Lady MacRobert using her own."

"As a consequence of her wonderful fighting response in the face of the tragic family disaster the whole world knows so well, the Court of the Lyon King of Arms decided to award to Lady MacRobert the signal honour of bestowing on her the right to carry the Coat of Arms of the Baronetcy of MacRobert. This includes the raising of her Banner on all occasions where she is present and of all the rights, privileges, salutations etc accorded to a Baronet. To establish this right the Lyon King changed her title from Lady MacRobert of Cawnpore and Cromar to Lady MacRobert of Douneside and Cromar. This is a unique honour in heraldic history for the Arms of a Baronet to be carried by a woman, and this is the first occasion to which public attention has been drawn to this wonderful distinction.

"The MacRobert Trust. There being now no Baronet left and Lady MacRobert being the sole representative of the family, she planned to preserve the traditions of the House of MacRobert of Douneside by the creation of the MacRobert Trust. In consequence of the nobility and scope of her plans, the Court of the Lyon King again granted a unique honour in the bestowal of a Coat of Arms for the MacRobert Trust. On this appear three winged Tigers heads emblematical of the flying record of the three MacRobert sons, and symbolic of Sir Alexander MacRobert's connection with India, and also of courage, which heraldically is exemplified by the Tiger. A pile driven into the top of the MacRobert Arms shows for the first time the flying wings in Heraldry. It will, I am sure, be a pleasure to all of you to know that as Senior Trustee of the MacRobert Trust, Mr William Heughan is entitled to raise the Banner of the Trust on all lawful occasions at which he is present."

The Trust's motto now became *Non Sibi Sed Partriae* – 'Not for Self but for Country'. Finally, in 1954, came the MacRobert Foundation, which was a grant making body with wide charitable aims. This was wound up in 1996.

A key figure in setting up the Trusts was William Heughan who, after first coming to Douneside to sing at Alasdair's 21st birthday celebration, became a loyal and valued aide whose skills, interests and expertise complimented Rachel's both intellectually and culturally. His particular influence though, was over the management of the farms and estate and his worth was recognised when he was appointed a trustee of each Trust. He helped her to earn the praise set out in the citation when Rachel was awarded the Medal of Honour from the National Society of New England Women. This recognised her as 'a good business woman interested in large scale farming and stock raising and in food production. Helper in national and public work and a philanthropist who has met the acid test of sorrow and been victorious'. It added that while her sons 'had the courage which dares', she had 'the courage which bears'.

William Heughan supported Rachel through all her triumphs and tragedies and when she died, he assumed the role of Chief Trustee.

During this time the Trust gave financial support to establish the MacRobert Arts Centre at Stirling, Scotland's first post-war university. To advance the cause of good architecture, a significant grant was awarded to Aberdeen University to regenerate its 15th and 16th century houses, breathing new life to the area surrounding St Machar's Cathedral and Kings College in Old Aberdeen.

The Trust also contributed funds to see the MacRobert Pavilion erected at Ingliston, the Royal Highland Agricultural Society's permanent show site on the outskirts of Edinburgh, where Rachel's cattle had been shown so successfully.

Following William Heughan's death in 1965 – he was buried close to Rachel at Douneside – the Trustees focused on improving the fabric of the estate and the farms. The administration of the Trusts was simplified and the offices moved from Douneside to Balmuir House in the village. This allowed for another new chapter in the life of the house that Mac had purchased as Burnside in 1888 as a home for his parents and brother and as a base for himself and Georgina on their trips home from India. Douneside was the place where his sons had spent an idyllic childhood and Rachel had provided generous hospitality to her guests. Now it became a holiday centre for serving and retired officers of the Armed forces and their families. At the same time, the Trusts formalised the policy on grant giving, and since then, successive Trustees and Administrators have dispersed funds to help a very large number of causes.

During his time as Administrator at the Trust, from 1985 until 1995, Lieutenant General Sir Robert Richardson travelled the length and breadth of the country. A key part of his job was to assess the appeals for donations that the Trusts received and to place his recommendations before the trustees for their approval.

In 1993, knowing that the Trust had never previously recognised any significant anniversary, Sir Bob suggested to the Chairman, Air Marshal Sir Richard Wakeford, that they should mark its Golden Jubilee.

There followed a year to remember. Queen Elizabeth, the Queen Mother, and the Duke of Kent sent messages of congratulation and the Trustees who wished the occasion to be remembered in the area long after the celebrations were over, presented local organisations with mementos. The main anniversary event was held over a weekend in July in a style reminiscent of Alastair's 21st birthday party.

The plans for the anniversary dinner were masterminded by Candy Richardson, Sir Bob's wife, who, with a willing band of helpers, transformed the MacRobert Hall in Tarland into a venue befitting the occasion. The lady guests were presented with a brooch depicting a Highland Cow, while the men received a goblet engraved with the MacRobert Trusts' coat of arms. But this was only the beginning of a memorable weekend.

The next day, the Military Band of the 1st Battalion the Royal Scots (The Royal Regiment) and the Grampian Police Pipe Band played for the guests at a buffet lunch at Douneside House. When estate employees and tenant farmers joined the merry throng for afternoon tea, the company heard the voice of Rachel played over the tannoy system in a recording of one of her wartime speeches. In it, she exhorted the women of Britain to rally to the cause in support of their men-folk. And in a moving tribute to their 'fairy godmother', to her boys who served their country, and to the MacRobert Trusts, the RAF mounted a display that looked both to the past and to the future. With typical accuracy, at precisely 4 p.m., a lone Spitfire flew over the Howe, followed by four GRI Tornados from XV Squadron which made mock attacks on Douneside. Then in stately fashion, Tornados from 43 and XV Squadrons flew in perfect formation over the House before the display came to a fitting end with the Tornado, 'MacRobert's Reply', roaring proudly overhead before disappearing high into the sky.

The following day, as members of the public enjoyed tea in the gardens, it was the turn of the Towie Pipe Band to entertain. The weekend is well remembered in the Howe, but it was not the end of the celebrations. In September, the RAF's crack display team, the Red Arrows, added its appreciation for the support offered by the MacRobert Trusts when it staged a flypast over Douneside. Later that month when the Duke of Kent, in his capacity as President of the RAF Benevolent Fund, visited Douneside and Alastrean House, he unveiled a wall plaque on a terrace. Nearby were a sundial and seats given by the RAF Benevolent Fund as a token of its gratitude for the Trusts' generosity in times of both peace and war.

The Trusts also marked this significant milestone in their history by making two major charitable donations. One went to the Children's Hospice Association in Scotland (CHAS), enabling it to open its first care centre for children with life-limiting disabilities and their families. At £2,000,000, this was the Trusts' largest-ever donation and thanks to it, the Rachel MacRobert Children's Hospice, known as Rachel House, was opened in Kinross.

Candy Richardson and the spouses of the Trustees at the time also came up with an inspirational idea to commemorate the MacRobert name in a more personal fashion. Marianne More-Gordon, whose work is acclaimed for its inventive combinations of texture, was commissioned to make three textile panels depicting the MacRobert story to hang in the hospice. Not only did the Trustees and their wives contribute to the cost of this work of art, but they also gave precious pieces of fabric to be used in its creation. Among these donors was Kay Boggis, Rachel's confidante and wife of that brave aviator who was captain of the first MacRobert's Reply. She gave material from an evening dress bequeathed to her by Rachel. The two outer panels of the work show Alastrean and Rachel House, while the one in the centre depicts the peace and beauty of Douneside with its rose-filled garden. It also shows three tigers flying away from the house: a poignant reminder of the lost MacRobert boys. In supporting the creation of Rachel House, the Trust has helped families to make the most of the precious time they have together in an atmosphere of love and laughter amidst the tears.

In a second magnanimous gesture that year, the Trust contributed to the establishment of the MacRobert Chair of Physics at Aberdeen

University, providing five annual donations of £50,000. The gift was inspired not only by Mac's thirst for knowledge and his links with the university but also by Rachel's achievements in the world of science.

In Tarland the Jubilee was marked by the construction of six new houses for pensioners and also the Leisure Centre which is available for use by the local community.

Major General John Barr succeeded Sir Bob as the Administrator. In 2001, the separate but closely associated Trusts were consolidated fully into a single new Trust by the Court of Session. This new simplified Trust bearing the family's name emerged with an easily understood mandate. None of the aims and objectives of the separate Trusts were lost in a move that marked a significant milestone in its history. So wide was the spectrum of charities and organisations that approached the MacRobert Trust for financial assistance, that the job took John and his wife June from some of the most impoverished areas of Britain to Buckingham Palace. They felt privileged to gain a balanced view of society and found the United Kingdom to be full of well-intentioned, good people working selflessly on behalf of those less fortunate than themselves. June remembers:

> There were so many interesting and compassionate visits. I recall visiting a charity for the homeless in the east end of London where we met an ex-serviceman. When he left the Army he fell on hard times and became homeless. The charity had taken him in, encouraging and enabling him to set up his own business importing meat. He was able to stay at the home until his business was established and then was rehoused.
>
> Another visit I remember well was to a drug rehabilitation centre. We were given a guided tour, but the doors were closed and locked as we went through to ensure everyone's safety. All concerned with the running of the charity were totally dedicated and involved in their work and the charity was able to demonstrate great success.
>
> We both enjoyed our time with the Trust. We both learnt so much. It was educational, enlightening and humbling, as well as exciting, made especially so by all the wonderful people we met during our travels and in our daily lives in and around Tarland.'

During John's term, he faced the responsibility of overseeing an estate of 7,500 acres at a time when the effects of the BSE and Foot and Mouth outbreaks were wreaking havoc across the countryside. He took, he says, a 'hands-on' approach to learning the business of managing the land. Friday afternoons would find him parked at roadsides and striding through fields with his mentor, for he took the view that the Common Agricultural Policy, the Access to the Countryside legislation and the changing laws on land tenure all presented opportunities to shape the estate for the future and to use the land in a better balanced, ecological way.

One of John's duties was to take part in the presentation, by Prince Philip, of the MacRobert Award, the United Kingdom's most prestigious prize for innovation in engineering. The award, which originally came with a prize of £25,000 and a gold medal, is now known as the Royal Academy of Engineering MacRobert Award and is worth £50,000. The innovative nature and at times simplicity of the projects that have won it over the years, from the 'Pipeline Pig' invented for the oil industry to the medical equipment manufacturer who succeeded in simplifying inhalers using chip technology, never ceased to impress John.

Over the years, a very large number of other charitable donations have been made to causes that reflect the interests of the MacRoberts: to people involved in agriculture, the Royal Air Force, and the Air Training Corps. The MacRobert name has graced gliders, bombers and fighter aircraft, life boats, hospitals and hospices, universities and colleges. In India where Mac made his fortune and his philanthropic works began, and in Scotland, which he never forgot, the memory of a family that in modern parlance 'made a difference' lives on.

Mac was a wise man who rose from humble beginnings, thanks to his fertile and inventive mind and his ability to absorb information. He not only built a business that was admired throughout the British Empire, but he also devoted his energies to improving the lives of his fellow men. The MacRobert Trust works in this spirit to this day.

Mac's brainchild, the British India Corporation, did not fare so well without him. In 1920, he had expressed doubts about India's readiness and willingness to accept such a huge conglomerate. Many did indeed, see the amalgamation of the companies as a means of concentrating control and viewed the change with suspicion and unease. In 1946, in a move that confirmed those fears, the British India Corporation with Sir Robert Menzies at the helm grew even bigger after taking over its rival Begg Sutherland. Begg Sutherland in its turn, owned ten important companies including two in the cotton industry, two in sugar and two in engineering.

But while the deal was regarded as quite a coup at the time, the new group's success was short-lived. On 15 August 1947, India became independent and the exodus of British and European mill owners began soon after. Local people now held positions as directors and shareholders in the BIC, whose capital in 1951 stood at $2,625,000. As minority shareholders, the Trust could no longer exert any influence and the remaining shares were sold. In 1981, the BIC was nationalised: it is now a Public Sector Undertaking of the Ministry of Textiles of the Government of India. Today only two of its businesses are operational: the woollen mills at Cawnpore and at Dhariwal, Mac's original enterprises.

The Trust of course, continues its work. Air Commodore Bob Joseph, who took over as Administrator in 2004, sums up its unique ethos:

> The MacRobert Trust covers so many different strands of business that it is easy to become pre-occupied with day-to-day issues. From time to time, certain events bring you down to earth and remind you of the reasons why we do what we do.
>
> There have been many of these in my time as Administrator. They range from the one-off events such as the 2004 commemoration of the 50th anniversary of Lady MacRobert's death with a small, but powerful ceremony at her graveside on the lawns of Douneside House, complete with a flypast of Tornado GR4 aircraft from No XV Squadron, Royal Air Force Lossiemouth, through to calendar events such as the annual Air Training Corps Lady MacRobert Trophy parade at Douneside House or the graduation ceremony and award of the Lady MacRobert Prize at the Royal Air Force College, Cranwell.

In their own way, each of these events, along with others, provide time for thought and reflection usually in a stunning setting, but the single event that will stay with us for many years to come was far simpler and far removed from any grandeur, but it offered no less a sense of occasion.

On Saturday 4 May 2013, my wife Jan and I stood with a group of around 100 local people and a small representative party from No XV(R) Squadron in a small clearing in the Gals Klint forest near Middelfart, Denmark. This spot, marked in the centre by a simple memorial stone containing the names of eight Royal Air Force airmen, was where Stirling bomber W7531, tail number LS-F, and the second aircraft to carry the name 'MacRobert's Reply', crashed on 18 May 1942 following a mine laying raid in the Danish Sound.

'Each year on 4/5 May, the Danish people commemorate the sacrifice made by British airmen and others in the struggle against Nazi Germany and the efforts to liberate Denmark from occupation. This small forest clearing is far from the grandeur of Douneside House, but it conveys no less powerful memories of Lady MacRobert's sad loss and the gift of £25,000 she gave to the Secretary of State for Air to buy a bomber to carry on her sons' work. This was barely a month after the loss of her third son, Sir Iain Workman MacRobert, on active service in June 1941. A bronze representative statue of the original Stirling bomber she funded, and which carried the name 'MacRobert's Reply', stands in the grounds at Douneside and is a daily reminder, but the opportunity to be in the clearing at Gals Klint was very special indeed.

'Later that same day, we stood at the Assistens Commonwealth War Graves Cemetery in Odense where the eight crew members were buried and later we joined several hundred people in placing lighted candles at the Odense City Cenotaph after a memorial service in the Church of Ansgar. Jan and I had vowed that we would attend the Danish ceremonies during our time with the MacRobert Trust in Tarland and I am delighted that we managed to do so in May 2013.'

Whilst Mac and Georgina could not produce heirs to the dynasty, they proved that endeavour and compassion for fellow man reap their own rewards. Mac and Rachel's boys did not live long enough to make their mark, but Rachel's defiance in the face of adversity ensured that they too left a legacy. Today the MacRobert Trust is the custodian of the lands for future generations: lands that Mac so wished to own and which Rachel came to love.

The Trust has remained faithful to the ideals that Mac, Georgina and Rachel lived by, through providing opportunities to those who need and deserve support and, just as importantly, by having faith in them. Thus their memory lives on.

Acknowledgements

One Christmas in the atmospheric surroundings of Fyvie Castle, I had a chance conversation with Major General John Barr, past Administrator of the MacRobert Trust. When I told him that I was hoping to write a book about the estates of the North East of Scotland and the families who ran them, he suggested that I should research the MacRoberts of Douneside and offered to arrange an introduction to his successor, Air Commodore Bob Joseph.

I harboured a doubt that anything might come of it, but at that time I did not know John Barr very well. The telephone duly rang the next morning and there was Bob with an invitation to come to Douneside. His generosity in making available information from the archives has allowed me insights into the family that I could never have gained elsewhere. Bob has suffered my years of research with great patience.

The 7th Marquess of Aberdeen and Temair also generously allowed access to the archives at the Haddo Estate Office. These detailed the circumstances of the transfer of the Aberdeen's lands to the MacRoberts, and helped me to understand the relationship between Lady Aberdeen and Lady MacRobert, so that I could present a balanced account of what happened.

He also introduced me to Simon Welfare, who, according to Lord Aberdeen, is the family's expert on the Gordons of Haddo in the 19th and 20th centuries. However, our initial pooling of facts became something more. Simon's rigorous editing of this book, his guidance and his gentle encouragement of this rookie writer, previously unknown to him, was way beyond the call of duty. Without this encouragement, help and advice, especially in the final throes of writing this book, the story would not be in the public domain today.

Gentlemen, thank you.

I am indebted to Rosemary Millington who, with great generosity of spirit, allowed me to read material that she had gleaned from her own previous research into the MacRobert family. This helped me to verify facts and to see some episodes from a different perspective.

With unfailing good humour, Vicky Duke at the MacRobert Trust has plied me with refreshments, and uncomplainingly, and with incredible patience, found every box in the archive that I have requested. She exudes a 'calm sough' at all times. June Armstrong, also at the Trust, has given willingly of her extensive knowledge of the MacRobert family, and I am grateful to Billy Shields for his information about the estate.

The lives of the three main characters in this story span a century from 1854 to 1954, and of necessity, particularly in the earlier chapters, I have had to rely on factual information gleaned from written material and occasionally the internet. Inevitably there have been discrepancies and where these arise I have done my best to verify the information. Aiding and abetting me have been numerous people from various bodies and organisations who with friendly efficiency have responded to my requests for information.

I am grateful to Dr Marion White and the Library Group at the Aberdeen Medico-Chirurgical Society, to Fiona Watson, archivist at NHS Grampian, and to Professor Neva Haites, and Professor Heather Wallace at the University of Aberdeen. The team librarian and staff of the local studies department at Aberdeen City Libraries and the staff at the Special Libraries and Archives, Library and Historic Collections at the University of Aberdeen provided me with information, as did the staff at the Special Collections Library at Edinburgh University.

The late Professor Mike Pittilo, Principal and Vice Chancellor of the Robert Gordon University, and his staff provided information on Robert Gordon's College, along with Henry Ellington, author of the book The Robert Gordon University – A History, and Penny Hartley, the archivist at Robert Gordon's College.

Thanks go too, to Jane Steven, former Secretary of the U.K. Committee for Dr Graham's Homes, Kalimpong, and to Rita McDonald, for her insight into life in India, her constant interest in this project, and for lending me Olivia in India.

But, as necessary as the factual information is, the story would not have come alive without the generosity of those who so willingly shared their personal memories. I have been delighted, at times humbled, and also astonished at the warm reception I have received from so many people. I could have spoken for hours to them all, so I hope they, too, enjoyed the time we spent together.

The recollections of Ian, Ann and Alice Anderson and Lorna McKechnie of the Friesian and Highland cattle enterprises respectively, have made my task much easier. Eddie Gillanders and Henry Durward shared their formidable knowledge of the Aberdeen Angus breed. Thank you Eddie for so willingly doing so. And what can I say Henry? Your memory of the animals in your care is virtually encyclopaedic. I was enthralled!

Vera and Norman Leslie's personal memories of working with Lady MacRobert were invaluable. I learned what it was like to work for the MacRobert enterprises after speaking to Fred and Helen Paterson, Hugh Brown and Bert Paterson: they brought those days to life. My thanks also, to Ethel Brown, Joy Whyte, and Peter Jamieson for their input and hospitality. Rob Blackhall shared his memories, along with Robert Dinnie and Ed Anderson who suggested I speak to Henry Gray. This led to a most enjoyable visit to hear Henry's recollections of Lady MacRobert.

Ian Booth shared memories, and those of his late father who was Lady MacRobert's accountant. Martyn R. Ford – Jones, Historian with XV Squadron RAF, and his wife Valerie generously allowed his photographs (from the Martyn R. Ford-Jones Collection) and information from their publications to be reproduced and willingly shared his extensive knowledge of the Squadron, the aircraft and those brave men who fly them.

The members of the Cromar History Group have encouraged me throughout my research. They have kindly permitted me to quote from minute books and records of proceedings held in the archives and have also shared their own knowledge. Thank you for taking such an interest.

Marianne More – Gordon generously gave her permission to reproduce the postcard of one of the textile hangings she designed for Rachel House. Pat Moir affected an introduction to Stephen Hart from Children's Hospice Association Scotland (CHAS) arranged for me to see round Rachel House to view the wall hangings and appreciate the wonderful work carried out there.

And finally, my thanks to the Administrators of the MacRobert Trust past and present, namely Sir Robert Richardson, Major General John Barr and Air Commodore Bob Joseph, and their wives, Candy, June and Jan. They have given me a privileged insight into its work and the ethos that guides it. Over the years, the Trust's charitable activities have ranged far and wide and I am well aware that my list of them is, to say the least, by no means comprehensive. Interested readers should consult the Trust's website: http://www.themacroberttrust.org.uk

All that said, any opinions and errors in these pages are mine alone.

Marion Miller

Bibliography

I am especially indebted to Zoë Yalland's *Boxwallahs, The British in Cawnpore 1857–1901*, published in 1994 by Michael Russell (Publishing Ltd.). This has proved an invaluable source, enabling me to verify information gleaned elsewhere and to gain insights into the industries of Cawnpore and the people who worked there. The author's family was among them: her grandfather, Arthur Butterworth, was the manager of the Cawnpore Woollen Mills. When Zoë's mother Ruby, the youngest of seven Butterworth children, was born, Georgina McRobert wanted to adopt her. The offer was declined, but Ruby was given the middle name Georgina in recognition of the gesture. And there is another family connection: Zoe Yalland's Aunt Kitty, her mother's sister, married Mac's nephew, Arthur Lilley.

3rd Statistical Account of Scotland, County of Aberdeen, Collins, 1960

Allardyce, John, *Bygone Days of Aberdeenshire*, The Central Press (John Milne), Aberdeen, 1913

Allen, Charles, ed., *Plain Tales from the Raj*, Readers Union, 1976

Allen, John R., *Farmers Boy*, Longman Group, 1975

Astor, Gavin, *The Tapestry of Tillypronie*, 1971

Chatterton, Eyre, *A History of the Church of Scotland in India*, SPCK 1924

Cromar History Group Archives

De Courcy, Anne, *The Viceroy's Daughters*, Weidenfeld & Nicolson, 2000

Douglas, O, *Olivia*, Thomas Nelson & Sons, 1929

Drummond, James, *Onward and Upward*, Aberdeen University Press, 1983

Ellington, Professor Henry, *The Robert Gordon University*, The Robert Gordon University, Aberdeen, 2002

Farquharson, Angus, *Finzean The Fair Place*, Ternan Publishing, 2008

Farquharson, Geoffrey, *Clan Farquharson A History*, Tempus Publishing, 2005

Farquharson-Lang, W.M., *The Manse and The Mansion*, Pentland Press, 1987

Fraser & Lee, ed, *Aberdeen 1800 – 2000*, Tuckwell Press, 2000

Gordon, Archie, *A Wild Flight of Gordons*, Weidenfeld & Nicolson, 1985

Graham, Cuthbert, *Portrait of Aberdeen and Deeside*, Robert Hale, 1980

Gunn, A.C., *The MacRobert Trusts 1943 –1993*, The MacRobert Trust, 1994

Keith, Alexander, *A Thousand Years of Aberdeen*, Aberdeen University Press, 1972

King, Peter, ed, *A Viceroy's India*, Sidgwick & Jackson, 1984

Levack, Iain, and Dudley, Hugh, *Aberdeen Royal Infirmary*, Bailliere Tindall, 1992

Minto, *James R., Graham of Kalimpong*, William Blackwood, 1974

Mitchell, Ian C., *The Douneside Story*, The MacRobert Trust, 1979

Morgan, Patrick, *Annals of Woodside and Newhills*, David Wyllie & Son, 1886

Pentland, Marjorie, *A Bonnie Fechter – The Life of Ishbel Marjoribanks, Marchioness of Aberdeen and Temair*, Jarrold & Sons, 1952

Reid, John C., *Mechanical Aberdeen*, Keith Murray Publishing, 1990

Smith, Alexander, ed, *A History of Aberdeenshire, Vol. 1*, Lewis Smith, Aberdeen, and William Blackwood & Sons, Edinburgh and London, 1875

Tangye, Derek, *Went the Day Well*, Michael Joseph, 1995

The Deeside Field, 2nd Series, No. 2, 1957

The Gordonian, June 1928

The Gordonian, June 1931

The MacRobert Trusts Golden Jubilee 1943–1993 Fly Past Souvenir Programme, The MacRobert Trust, 1993

Thornton-Kemsley, Colin, *Bonnet Lairds*, Standard Press, Montrose, 1972

Webster, Jack, *Jack Webster's Aberdeen*, Birlinn, 2007

Index

Aberdeen, William, 2nd Earl of, 146
Aberdeen Angus, 48, 167, 175–178,
    194
Aberdeen, City of, 11–12, 14–21, 23,
    25, 29, 31, 34, 36, 41, 44, 69,
    71–72, 76–77, 85, 90, 117–119,
    122, 125, 137, 157, 160, 165, 169,
    172
Aberdeen Chamber of Commerce,
    121
Aberdeen City Libraries, 193
Aberdeen County Nursing
    Association, 148
Aberdeen Medico-Chirurgical Society,
    193
Aberdeen & Temair, 1st Marquess of,
    79, 82, 118, 127–128, 146–154,
    157, 169–170, 180, 192
Aberdeen & Temair, 7th Marquess of,
    192
Aberdeen & Temair, Marchioness of,
    79, 82, 146–154, 169, 192
Aberdeen, University of, 73–75, 81,
    118, 121, 180, 184, 193
Aberdeenshire, 1, 11–12, 15, 19, 41,
    46, 48, 54, 79–80, 92, 98, 132,
    147–148, 154, 164, 180, 196, 197
Aboyne, 80, 149, 155, 162, 172, 174
Afghanistan, 7, 26–27, 58, 96–103,
    108
Agricultural College of Cawnpore, 67,
    120
Air Forces Memorial, Runnymede,
    136
Akali Movement, 116

Alamein Agricultural Training Group,
    163–164
Alastrean House, 132, 145, 154–156,
    165, 181, 186
Alexandra, Queen, 81
Allahabad, 30, 42, 81, 111, 120
Allardyce family, 175
Allen, Charles T., 22, 118
Allen, Sir George 22, 24, 30, 65, 111
Allen, George Berney, 22, 24, 36, 84,
    85, 88, 92, 125
Allen, Harry 22
Allenvale Cemetery, Aberdeen, 20, 69,
    71, 118
Anderson, Alice, 155, 165, 172, 194
Anderson, Ann, 194
Anderson, Ed, 194
Anderson, Ian, 155, 167, 194
Anderson, Norman, 155, 165, 172
Armstrong, June, 193
Arnott, Neil, 18, 69
Auchlossan, 79

BA Eagle aeroplane, 130, 143
Baird, Margaret, 156
Ballater, 80, 155, 178
Banchory Devenick, 19, 46
Bangalore, 98
Barclay, J.W., 79
Barr, Major General John, 187, 188,
    192, 195
Barr, June, 187, 195
Beck, Rev. H.W., 132
Begg Sutherland, 189
Blackhall, Alexander J., 176

Blackhall, Rob, 194
Blackhall, William, 162
Boggis, Kay, 139, 186
Boggis, Peter, 138–139, 141
Bombay, 29–30, 37, 40, 67–69, 98, 130
Booth, Ian, 194
Brest raid, 139
British Aeromodellers Association, 180
British India Corporation (BIC), 12, 14, 109–111, 113–115, 118, 122, 128–130, 133–134, 182, 188–189
British Red Cross Society, 148
Broadford Mill, 14–15, 25
Brock, Charles Edmund, 125
Brown, Ethel, 194
Brown, Hugh, 167, 194
Buchan, Anna Masterton (O. Douglas), 29, 36
Burnside, Tarland, 184
Butler, Sir Harcourt, 108, 119
Butterworth, Alfred, 34, 36, 196
Butterworth, Kitty, 34, 196
Butterworth, Polly, 34
Butterworth, Ruby, 34, 196

Calcutta, 17, 64, 67, 76
Calcutta, Bishop of, 41
Cambridge, 125–127, 174
Cambridge University Air Squadron, 126
Carnegie, Andrew, 81
Carnousie House, Forglen, 92
Cawnpore, 13, 16, 20, 21–30, 34–37, 38–46, 49–50, 55, 66–67, 70–78, 85, 88, 97, 99, 101–114, 118–120, 122, 124, 126, 129, 133, 182–183, 189, 196

Cawnpore Agricultural College, 67, 120
Cawnpore Club, 35
Cawnpore Tent Club, 36
Cawnpore Rifle Club, 36
Cawnpore Volunteers' Rifles, 35–37
Cawnpore Woollen Mill, 16, 21, 22, 24, 26, 28, 34, 46, 78, 85, 97, 105, 107–109, 111, 122, 189, 196
Chamber of Commerce of the British Empire, 64, 84
Chamber of Commerce, United Provinces, 55
Christ Church, Cawnpore, 41–42, 77, 118
Christ Church School, Cawnpore, 41–42
Claremont Laundry, Aberdeen, 20, 31
Clark, Sir James, 18, 80
Clark, Sir John, 80
Cocker, Annie (Georgina's niece), 69
Cocker's Roses, Aberdeen, 169
Collie, J. Younger 118
Colney Park, St Albans, 93
Connaught, Duchess of, 58
Connaught, Duke of, 57–58
Cooper Allen & Co., 21–22, 30, 46, 60, 65, 98, 111, 113
Cooper, William, 21–22, 24, 30, 42, 60, 111, 113, 118
Coutts, John of Auchtercoull, 146
Cowan, Rev. Professor, 118
Cowe, Geordie, 175
Crerar, Group Captain Finlay, 154
Cripps, Sir Richard Stafford, 180
Cromar Estate, 146, 149–154
Cromar Hall, Tarland, 157–158
Cromar History Group, 194
Cromar Nursing Association, 180
Cruickshank, Dr John, 75

Cudworth, Marjory, 84–85, 168
Curzon of Kedleston, 1st Marquess, 55–60
Cushnie, 94

Daily Telegraph, Lucknow, 39, 64, 72, 107
Deeside District Committee, 94–96
Deeside Field Club, 90
Delhi, 54–56, 61, 87–88
Delhi Durbar (1877), 55, 56, 58
Delhi Durbar (1902/3), 54–61
Delhi Durbar (1911), 55, 87, 88
Denmark, 135, 141, 174, 190
Dhariwal New Egerton Mill, 19, 66, 102, 106–107, 109, 116–117, 122, 189
Dinnet, Muir of, 146
Dinnie, Robert, 194
Dodd, Air Vice-Marshal Frank, 140
Donington Park, 126
Douneside House & Estate, 12, 13, 33, 45–53, 69, 71–78, 79–80, 84, 87–88, 90, 92–94, 100–104, 125–128, 130–135, 139, 146, 151, 155, 162–164, 166–179, 181–186, 189–190, 192, 197
Dr Graham's Homes, 43–45, 76, 193
Dufferin & Ava, 1st Marquess, 27, 40, 101
Dufferin & Ava, 1st Marchioness of, 40–41
Duke, Vicky, 192
Duncan, Reverend J, 178
Dundee Courier, 156, 159
Durward, Henry, 175, 194

Edinburgh University, 193
Edward, VII, King, 54, 57–58, 60, 81

El Gamil, Egypt, 143
Elgin Cotton Spinning & Weaving Company, 109
Elgin Mills, 109–110
Elizabeth, Princess, 148
Elizabeth II, Queen, 180–181
Ellington, Professor Henry, 193
Empire Engineering Co., 110
Evans, W. G., 75

Farquharson, Andrew, 104
Farquharson, Robert, 79–80
Flamborough Head, Yorkshire, 135
Ford-Jones, Martyn R., 194
Ford-Jones, Valerie, 194
Fowler, Vaughan, 130
Friesian cattle, 92, 125, 165, 171–173, 175, 179

Galsklint, Funen, Denmark, 141, 190
Gandhi, Mohandas Karamchand, 128
George V, King, 85, 87
George VI, King, 131, 148
Georgina McRobert Fellowship, 73–76
Georgina McRobert Memorial Hospital, Cawnpore, 75, 122, 130, 133
Georgina McRobert Memorial Tower, 77
Ghose, Dr Tarunendu, 75
Gillanders, Eddie, 194
Glasgow, 144–145, 153, 166
Glasgow Bulletin, 153
Glassel Estate, 92
Glenbuchat, 79
Glen Tanar, 92
Gneisenau, 139
Gordon, Maria Ogilvie, 85, 132

Gordon Highlanders, 58, 127, 149
Gray, Henry, 162, 194
Gray, Sir Henry, 118
Gourlay, W.A, 76
Grenoble University, 126
Guisachan Estate, 147

Haddo House, 147, 153
Haddo House Estate, 150, 152, 192
Haites, Professor Neva, 193
Halifax bomber, 139
Harris, Air Vice Marshall Sir Arthur, 134
Hart, Stephen, 194
Hartley, Penny, 193
Hawker Hurricane, 134, 141–142, 145, 163, 180
Hector, Dr William, 149
Heughan, William, 127–128, 132, 143, 144, 155, 158–159, 162, 167, 169, 174, 175–176, 183–184
Highland cattle, 173–175, 194
Hill, Eric, 140
Horsfall, Charles, 90
House of Cromar, 79, 125, 127, 145–154
House of Lords, 94–95.
Howe of Cromar, 49, 145–146, 149, 152, 165

Ilbert, Sir Courtney, 62
Indian Aviation Development Company, 130–131, 133.
Indian Industrial Commission, 63, 120
Indian Mutiny, 7, 21–24, 26, 37, 41, 59, 66–67, 105, 112
Indian National Congress, 63, 64, 128
International Council of Women, 148

International Women's Day National Committee, 179
Irish Industries Association, 148
Irish Motor Racing Club, 126

Jalalabad, 102, 104
Jamieson, Peter, 194
Jamieson, Thomas, 117
Jeffs, Sergeant Duncan, 141
Johnson, Sammy, 106
Jones, Gavin, 21, 22, 24, 41, 110–111, 113
Joseph, Bob, Air Commodore, 189–190, 192, 195
Joseph, Jan, 195

Khan, Habibullah, Amir of Afghanistan, 96–104
Khan, Khaligdad, 101
Khudaganj, 105
Khyber Pass, 27, 98
Khyber Rifles, 98
Kipling, Rudyard, 22, 40, 105
Kirkman, Nell, 34
Kitchener, Earl, 60, 90
Knowehead, Easter, 163
Knowehead, West, 175
Koblenz, 126

Lalimli Club, 34–35, 55
Lalimli Dictionary, 26, 28
Lalimli trademark, 25–26, 28, 57, 88
Lancaster bomber, 140
La Touche, Sir James, 41, 56
La Touche, Lady, 41, 56
Legislative Council, Agra & Oudh, 55, 120
Leslie, Norman, 166–167, 194
Leslie, Vera, 155, 156, 166, 194

Lilley, Arthur, 34, 88, 122, 129, 196
Lloyd George, David, 87
Lockhart, Miss J., 75
Lord Lyon King of Arms, 183
Low, Rev. William Marshall, 13, 132
Luton airport, 13, 131

McArthur, John, 132, 163
McCaw, John, 132
McClaughry, Air Vice Marshall
    Wilfred, 143
McCracken, Capt., 98
McDonald, Rita, 193
McFarlane, Peter, 176, 182
McKechnie, John, 174–175
McKechnie, Lorna, 194
McKechnie, W.W., 161
MacRobert Arts Centre, Stirling, 13,
    184
MacRobert Farms (Douneside) Ltd,
    177, 182
MacRobert, Georgina (Porter), 14, 18,
    20, 22, 28–35, 37, 39–49, 51,
    53–62, 64, 67–78, 80–82, 87–88,
    118, 121–122, 130, 133, 151, 155,
    168, 184, 190–191, 196
McRobert, Helen, 19, 47–51, 69, 78
McRobert John, 16, 19, 47, 48,
    50–51, 53, 94
McRobert, Johnny, 47, 50, 78, 79
MacRobert Memorial Hall, Tarland,
    18, 143, 157–160, 176, 182, 185
MacRobert Pavilion, Ingliston, 13,
    184
MacRobert, Rachel (née Workman),
    12, 14, 18, 22, 82–94, 102–104,
    113–115, 118, 122–124, 126–133,
    135–139, 141–146, 151, 153–175,
    177–187, 190–191

MacRobert Reply Association, 145
MacRobert Sir Alasdair, 13, 88, 90,
    92, 93, 124–134, 142–143, 150,
    154, 160, 162–163, 168, 171,
    182–183
MacRobert, Sir Alexander ('Mac'),
    passim.
MacRobert, Sir Iain, 13, 22, 88,
    92–93, 124, 126, 129, 135–138,
    142, 180, 182, 190, 197
MacRobert, Sir Roderic, 13, 88, 93,
    124–129, 132–136, 138, 142, 144,
    180, 182
MacRobert Trusts & Trustees, 5, 11,
    13, 19, 139, 140, 150, 151, 154,
    157–160, 163, 165–166, 169–170,
    172, 175, 181–190, 195, 197
MacRobert's Reply, 12, 13, 137–143,
    145, 165, 181, 185–186, 190–191
Madras, 81–82, 151
Malta, 144
Margaret, Princess, 148
Marischal College, Aberdeen, 18, 81,
    118
Marshall's Flying School, Cambridge,
    127
Mary, Queen, 148, 153
Maxwell, Hugh, 21, 41, 110
Mechanics's Institute, Aberdeen,
    17–18, 69
Melgum Estate, 91–92, 132, 163,
    167, 175
Menzies, Sir Robert, 129, 132–133,
    189
Meston, Sir James, 76, 124
Miller, James, 97–98, 102
Millington, Rosemary, 192–193
Minto, 4th Earl of, 97
Mitchell, Reginald, 180

Moir, Pat, 194
More-Gordon, Marianne, 186, 194
Mosul, Iraq, 134–135, 142
Mountbatten, Lord Louis, 180
Mozarteum, Salzburg, 133
Muir Mill, Cawnpore, 20–21, 27, 106, 110

National Society of New England Women, 163, 184
Nehru, Jawaharlal, 128
New Brunswick, Canada, 19, 47, 100
New Egerton Woollen Mill, 28, 46, 102, 106, 108–109, 115–116

Oban sales, 174–175
Ogg, Gavin, 175
'Operation Catechism', 140
'Operation Oiled', 139–140

Pandit, Mr, 124
Paterson, Bert, 169, 194
Paterson, Fred 174, 194
Paterson, Helen, 174, 194
Pathé, 143
Pendjeh, 26–27
Pentland, Lady Marjorie, 82, 151, 153, 197
Pentland, Lord, 82
Perth Bull Sales, 175–177
Peshawar, 103
Peterhead, 140
Philip, Dr James, 75
Philip, Prince, 180, 188
Pioneer newspaper, 22, 30, 65, 106
Pittilo, Professor Mike, 193
Porter, Annie, 20
Porter, Christina, 20
Porter, Mary, 20

Porter, William, 20
Pratt, Mr, 89, 168
Prestwick, 98

RAF Coningsby, 140
RAF Lossiemouth, 139–140, 181, 189
RAF Volunteer Reserve, 126
Rachel House, 186, 194
Ranna Farm, 93, 165, 166–167, 176
Rawalpindi, 27, 86, 101
Redhill, Surrey, 126
Redhill Flying Club, 131
Reid, Air Vice Marshall, 134
Reid, Duncan, 176
Reid, Edward, 93–95
Reid, Flight Lieutenant Bill, VC, 165–166, 176
Reid, Sir James, 18
Reid, Walter A., 162
Richards & Co, 14, 15, 25, 117
Richardson, Lady, 169, 185–186, 195
Richardson, Lieutenant – General Sir Robert, 169, 184, 185–186, 187, 195
Ricketts, Reverend, 178–179
Ripon, 1st Marquess, 62–63
Robert Gordon University, 193
Robert Gordon's College, Aberdeen, 17–18, 157, 160–162, 179, 193
Roberts, Frederick, 1st Earl, 105–6, 112
Roberts, Sir Abraham, 105
Robertson, Clan, 115, 154, 162
Rollo, Robert Leslie, 161–162
Roorkee Engineering College 120
Rosenorn-Lehn, Baron C, 174
Royal Academy of Engineering MacRobert Award, 188
Royal Agricultural Show, 174, 176

Royal Air Force, 13–14, 126–127, 130–131, 134–135, 137–138, 140, 142–146, 154, 157, 163, 178–179, 181, 185–186, 194
Royal Highland Show, 173–176, 184
Royal Infirmary & Lunatic Asylum, Aberdeen, 122
Royal Northern Agricultural Society, 167, 179
Royal Scots, 129, 185
Russian Air Regiment, 142

St John's Ambulance Association, 120
St John's College, Cambridge, 126
Salvation Army, 144
Scharnhorst, 139
Scotland's Gardens Scheme, 147–148
Scottish Chamber of Agriculture, 179
Scottish Women's Hospital for War Service, 121
Shand, William, 175
Sheiling, The, 28, 30–33, 42, 57, 76
Shields, Billy, 193
Siegfried, André, 62
Sinclair, Sir Archibald, 137–138, 141–142
Skoda factory, Pilsen, 139
Smith, Sir George Adam, 118
South Kensington Museum, 20
Spitfire, 137, 140, 180, 185
Stanstead House, Caterham, Surrey, 127, 132
Statesman newspaper, Calcutta, 17, 98–99, 119
Steven, Jane, 193
Stewart, Colonel John, 111–113
Stirling bomber, 138–141, 163, 180, 190

Stoneywood Paper Mills, 16, 18–19, 25, 85, 121
Stoneywood Useful Knowledge Association, 121
Strathcona, 1st Baron, 81
Suffragette movement, 84, 89–91, 158, 179

Tarland, 1, 11, 13, 46, 72, 80, 90, 91, 93–95, 104, 132, 143, 145–50, 155, 157–160, 162, 166–170, 176, 178, 180–182, 185, 187, 190
Tarland Golf Club, 155
Tarland Lodge, 91, 146, 148–150
Tarland Red Cross Committee, 149
Tarland School, 148, 170, 178
Tarland Welfare Trust, 158–159
Technical Institute, Cawnpore, 122
The Aeroplane magazine, 131
The Scotsman, 151, 159
The Week's Good Cause, 144
Thornton Kemsley, Colin, 164–165, 197
Tirpitz, 139–140
Trinity College, Cambridge, 125
Trondheim fjord, 139

Union Works, Aberdeen, 18
Upper India Chamber of Commerce, 42, 64, 85,105–106, 119–120
Upper Provinces Flying Club, Cawnpore, 126

Vaux, Peter, 136
Viceroy's Trophy air race, 130
Victoria, Queen, 18, 27, 49, 58–59, 62, 80
Victorian Order of Nurses, 148

Wakeford, Air Marshal Sir Richard, 185
Wakeford, Lady, 169
Wallace, Professor Heather, 193
Watson, Fiona, 193
Watson, Sir Logie, 85, 98, 100–104, 122
Welfare, Simon, 192
Wellington bomber, 138
West Town, 92, 93–96
Westcott, Foss, 41–42, 43
Westcott, George, 41–43
White, Dr Marion, 193
Whyte, Joy, 194
'Wings for Victory' campaign, 144–145

Women's National Health Association, Ireland, 148
Woolmanhill Hospital, Aberdeen, 122
Workman, Fanny, 82–83, 85, 166
Workman, Rachel, see MacRobert, Rachel
Workman, William, 82–83, 85–87, 166
World War I, 74, 100, 107, 127–128, 141, 148–149
World War II, 12, 75, 136, 137–45, 157, 163, 178

Yalland, Zoe, 21, 196
York, Duchess of, 148